RELYING
ON THE
HOLY SPIRIT

D1157381

RELYING
ON THE
HOLY SPIRIT

CHARLES
STANLEY

THOMAS NELSON PUBLISHERS
Nashville • Atlanta • London • Vancouver

Published in Nashville, Tennessee, by Thomas Nelson, Inc.

The Bible version used in this publication is THE NEW KING JAMES VERSION. Copyright © 1979, 1980, 1982, Thomas Nelson, Inc., Publishers.

ISBN 0-7852-7260-7

Printed in the United States of America.
11 12 13 14 15 — 02 01 00 99

CONTENTS

THE SPIRIT-FILLED LIFE IS FOR EVERY BELIEVER

The Spirit-filled life. In all likelihood, these words evoke one of three responses in you:

You may say, "I don't know what you're talking about." If that's your response, you aren't alone. Many people don't know much about the Holy Spirit, and they know less about how He works in the life of every Christian.

You may say, "Oh, I'm not sure I want anything to do with the Holy Spirit. Everything I've heard about the Holy Spirit seems divisive or too emotional for me." If that's your response, I have encouragement for you. If you are a genuine born-again Christian, you have a relationship with the Holy Spirit, whether you have acknowledged Him or not. Furthermore, *He* is not divisive or invasive. People may be, but He is not.

You may say, "Oh, yes! The Spirit-filled life is the most wonderful life a person can know. I wouldn't trade the Spirit-filled life for all the riches in the world or for any other experience or state of being!" If that's your response, I say "amen"—so be it. The Spirit-filled life is the only way for a Christian to experience all that God has for a person to be, say, and do. It is life to the fullest, the true abundant life that Jesus promised. (See John 10:10.)

The Spirit-filled life is not based on emotions, although you are likely to feel various emotions as the Spirit works in you and through you to produce the character of Christ Jesus and to replicate the ministry of Christ Jesus in your life and the world.

The Spirit-filled life is also not something that a person can study from afar. The Spirit-filled life is experienced. It is lived out by real people in real life facing real, and sometimes difficult, circumstances and situations.

The Spirit-filled life is marked by purpose, power, and effectiveness. It is not something that you do, but something that you are because of who is living and working inside you. God desires for each of His children to live a Spirit-filled life, and He expects you to be led by the Spirit on a daily basis.

Beyond Adequate

Many Christians are content to live an adequate Christian life. They believe that if they go to church, read their Bible occasionally, and say their prayers once in a while, they are all right with God. Occasionally, they volunteer to serve others in a particular way—perhaps as an usher, a member of a church committee, or a home visitor on an evangelism team—and they consider that ministry as above the norm.

Let me challenge you today. God doesn't call you or anyone to just an adequate Christian life. He desires to have a daily walking-and-talking relationship with you in which you experience His presence, trust Him for wisdom, courage, and strength, and rely on Him for results—at every step you take, every decision you make, every conversation you have, and every thought you think. The Lord desires to live within you. He desires to communicate to you and through you. He desires to live out His life through your expression of it—a perfect blending of His perfection and your unique talents, traits, and personality.

There is no such thing as an average Christian life. Either you are living a vibrant Spirit-filled life, or you aren't. You are in forward motion or in a pause position. You are living in the fullness of the Holy Spirit, or you aren't.

Make a decision today to choose the Spirit-filled life. That's within your prerogative and will to do. God will not force Himself on you or force Himself to operate within you. He works by invitation only. He won't overstep the boundaries of your will.

Lay Aside Your Preconceptions

You likely have some preconceptions about the Holy Spirit and how He works within a person's life. I encourage you to lay them aside and approach these lessons with a wide-open heart and mind. You can learn and experience something here. But you can't and won't unless you are willing to be changed in your inner person.

Reflect on these questions as you prepare for this study:

- *When I hear the phrase "Spirit-filled life," what comes to my mind?*

  _____

  _____

- *Am I open to knowing and experiencing more of the Holy Spirit in my life?*

  _____

  _____

- *Do I want more out of my relationship with Christ Jesus than I currently am experiencing?*

  _____

  _____

WHY WE NEED THE HOLY SPIRIT IN OUR LIVES

Most of us have no difficulty admitting, "I need Jesus Christ in my life." We recognize that we are sinful creatures by nature and that we must have the sacrificial, substitutionary, all-sufficient atonement made possible by Christ Jesus and His shed blood on the cross of Calvary if we are to experience forgiveness for our sins and to receive eternal life. Yes, we need Christ.

Most of us have no difficulty admitting, "I need God the Father in my life." We recognize Him as our all-powerful, ever-present, everlasting, sovereign, and holy Creator. Jesus Christ came into the world so that we might be restored to a full and intimate relationship with our heavenly Father, who in His infinite love desires to bless us as His children. Yes, we need God the Father. In many ways, we need Christ Jesus in our lives because of our need for a relationship with the Father.

But do we need the Holy Spirit? Let me assure you, we need the Holy Spirit in our lives just as much as we need a relationship with our heavenly Father and with His Son, Jesus Christ.

The Holy Spirit is part of the holy Trinity—Father, Son, and

Holy Spirit. You need Him just as much as you need Father and Son. In fact, the Holy Spirit makes possible your ongoing Christian life and enables you both to experience Christ and to have a relationship with the Father. The Holy Spirit enables you to have a sense of victory in your Christian walk. You need Him at work in you and through you if you are to fulfill your earthly destiny in Christ and become the person that the Father created you to be.

A Perspective on Feelings and Experiences

Many people claim to have had an experience with the Holy Spirit. Usually, they are referring to an initial experience—perhaps called a baptism in the Spirit—or to one or more spiritual high moments in their lives in which they felt His presence or experienced the power of God in an unusually strong way.

The fact is, all Christians have had an experience with the Holy Spirit. Otherwise, they really aren't Christians.

For a proper understanding of who the Holy Spirit is and how He works in our lives, we must go to God's Word. We can't base our relationship with the Holy Spirit on feelings or experiences.

Ultimately, feelings are unreliable. They change with the tides of human circumstances. Many factors contribute to our feelings. Experiences, too, are locked into time. We may have an experience on one day, and then not have a similar experience for weeks, months, years, or ever. In sharp contrast, the Word of God is lasting and true. It is a sure foundation for our believing and our behaving.

Some people have been taught erroneously about the Holy Spirit. I know people who seem to have taken just one phrase or one verse out of the Bible and built an entire theology of the Holy Spirit on it. We must have the whole counsel of God's Word on the subject of the Holy Spirit if we hope to have a full understanding of Him and a fuller experience with Him.

As in all areas of study, we err if we base our believing on one isolated concept. Truth in God's Word is expressed repeatedly. Verses build upon verses to create the whole meaning of God's message to us. Our perspective is limited—and in error—unless we take in the whole of God's truth.

In this study guide, you will find that I refer repeatedly to some passages of the Bible. I will be asking you to focus on particular aspects of the verse at each reading and to see how the various verses are connected in meaning.

I encourage you to make notes in the margins of your Bible as you work your way through this study guide. Note cross-references and jot down the insights God gives to you. It is much more important to write these notes in your Bible than to write in this study guide. That way your insights will be available to you as your read your Bible regularly through the years. Places are also provided, however, for you to make notes here.

Keys to This Study

Periodically, you will be asked one or more of these questions:

1. What new insights have you gained?
2. Have you ever had a similar experience?
3. How do you feel about this?
4. In what ways are you feeling challenged in your spiritual walk?

Insights

An insight might be considered an "aha" moment—a time when the meaning of a passage becomes crystal clear to you. This may happen even if you have read, studied, or meditated on a particular verse or passage many times. God is forever revealing new levels of meaning to us as we grow into maturity in Christ Jesus. He delights in giving us deeper spiritual insights as we are ready to receive them and act on them.

Ask God to reveal new insights to you as you read His Word. That's a prayer I believe God will answer every time!

Insights are usually very personal, and they generally relate to your experience, either past or current. This is one way in which God's Word is always timely, even as it is eternal.

I encourage you to write down your insights in as much detail as you can. Often, just in the writing, you'll have additional insights. In fact, as you write, you may have a keen awareness of the Holy Spirit prompting you to think, respond, or feel in a new direction. Then, too, if you have your insights in written form, you are much more likely to recall them in the future. You may have forgotten your impressions or insights temporarily, but when you see a note that you have written, you are reminded of God's truth at work in your life. Also, you tend to have more insights if you expect them and record them in a very intentional way. God speaks as you open your spiritual ears and eyes to Him.

In addition to places where I ask, "What new insights do you have?" there are a number of times in this study when you will find Scriptures under the headings "What the Word Says... What the Word Says to Me." These are places for you to record your spiritual insights.

Experiences

Each of us comes to God's Word with a unique background. What we read is filtered to some degree by our experiences. Our perspective on life—our frame of reference—is based to a great degree on our experiences. You no doubt have said, "I've seen that spiritual truth of the Bible at work in my life."

The more we see the Bible as related to our personal experiences, the more the Bible encourages, convicts, and challenges us. As we change our thinking and behaving to line up with the Bible, we are transformed in our spirits.

If we have only experience as the basis for our worldview—our perspective—we are very limited and can easily fall into error. We ultimately must have the Bible as our frame of reference. God's Word—every verse of it—applies to us. We can use our experiences to confirm to us that the Bible is true, but we must conform our behavior so that it lines up with God's Word and becomes evidence to others that the Bible is true.

As you take note of your experiences, you will likely see how the Lord has been at work in your life all along. Your faith grows when you see the Lord at work, and so does your awareness of His presence. Even if you are doing this study on your own, I encourage you to talk to others about your spiritual walk with God. Allow others to learn from you even as you learn from them.

Emotional Responses

You have not only an emotional response to the Lord but also an emotional response to His Word. No one emotional response is right or more valid than another when it comes to the way we feel about particular passages in the Bible. Your emotions may change slightly each time you read a particular passage. You may be frightened or puzzled by something you read, and at a later reading, you may be comforted and assured by the same passage. Furthermore, another person reading the same passage may have a different response altogether.

If emotions vary over time, and if we can't rely on emotions, why take note of them? First, we are healthier people if we face our emotions and learn to share them with others. Second, when we confront our emotions, we often see with new understanding how the Lord is working in us and how He may desire to work. For example, if you are perplexed by something you read, and you openly admit that to yourself, you are putting yourself into a position to request and to receive God's wisdom. But if you read through a passage and aren't aware of your feelings about it, you are far less likely to engage in the further study necessary to have your questions answered.

God created you with emotions. He knows that you feel certain ways toward Him, toward others, and toward His Word. He desires for you to be in touch with your feelings about these important areas of your life.

As you meet with others to study the Holy Spirit, stay focused on what the Bible says. As healthy as it is to share emotions, it is unwise to get locked into emotions or to make your Bible study time a "feel good" or "let's talk about how we feel" sharing session.

We must always be aware of any tendency to insist that others feel the same as we feel. Give each person in the group the freedom to feel what he or she feels without any pressure or a put-down attitude from other members.

Challenges

God intends for us to have insights into His Word, recall certain experiences, and face our emotions for a reason—to apply His Word to our lives and to share Him with others. There is no point in engaging in a Bible study, discussing past experiences, or exploring your feelings unless you might grow personally and you might encourage growth in others.

As you read and study God's Word, stop periodically and ask yourself, What does God desire to do in me and through me? Be aware of areas in your life that the Lord desires to change or build upon. Be aware of new directions He may be prompting you to pursue. God desires to get you into His Word so He can get His Word into you, and in turn, so you can share His Word with others. Real spiritual growth comes as you understand and apply God's Word to your personal life and relationships.

You likely will have opportunities to discuss what you learn in this study. Be bold in sharing with others how the Lord is working in your life.

If you don't have someone with whom to discuss your insights, experiences, emotions, and challenges, find someone. Perhaps you can start a Bible study in your home. Perhaps you can talk to your pastor about organizing Bible study groups in your church. There is much you can learn on your own. But there is much more to be learned as you become part of a small group that desires to grow in the Lord and to understand His Word more fully. That is how the body of Christ is built up.

Keep the Bible Central

I encourage you again to keep the Bible central to your study. Come to God's Word with an open heart and mind, expecting to be nourished and refreshed. Expect to come away with something from God each time you open the Bible.

Prayer

I also encourage you to begin and end each Bible study session in prayer. Ask the Lord to open your spiritual ears so you can hear what He has to say to you. Ask the Lord to open your understanding so you can learn all that He desires to teach you. Ask Him to open your spiritual eyes so you can see the direction He wants you to take. Very specifically, ask the Lord to give you insights, to bring to your remembrance past experiences that reinforce for you the truth of God's Word, and to help you clarify your emotions.

As you end a Bible study session, ask the Lord to seal to your heart what you have learned so that you will never forget it, and so that it will take root in your life and make you more like Jesus Christ. Ask the Lord for courage to do what He has challenged you to do. Pray for boldness to be faithful to Him always and to share your life in Him with others as often as possible.

And now, let me ask you,

- *What new insights about the Holy Spirit do you hope to gain from this study?*

  _____

  _____

- *Is there a past experience with the Holy Spirit that is troubling to you? Comforting to you?*

  _____

  _____

- *How do you feel about the Holy Spirit right now?*

  _____

  _____

- *Are you open to the possibility that God will lead you into a deeper and more meaningful relationship with Him?*

  _____

  _____

LESSON 2

WHO EXACTLY IS THE HOLY SPIRIT?

Have you ever seen a child stare in wide-eyed wonder as she listens to a new story? That's the way many people are when it comes to the Holy Spirit. They don't have a clue to His true identity or how He works in the life of every Christian. The Holy Spirit is a mystery to them.

Wide-eyed wonder is not a bad response to have to the Holy Spirit. Certainly, the Holy Spirit should inspire our awe, our wonder, our adoration. But the Holy Spirit does not desire to be a puzzle. He desires to reveal Himself to us and to be known by us.

Who, then, is the Holy Spirit? That's the focus of this lesson.

The Holy Spirit Is a Person

One of the keys to your understanding about the Holy Spirit lies in your recognition that the Holy Spirit is not an "it"; He is a person.

Have you ever been asked, "Are you filled with the Holy Spirit? Do you have the Holy Spirit?" There is only one set of answers: yes or no. You can't have a little bit of the Holy Spirit. Either you have been filled by Him, or you haven't.

You can't have had Him once, but not have Him now. Either you have Him, or you've never had Him.

The error tends to come because we think of the Holy Spirit as a force, a power, an event, an experience, a manifestation.

I once had this view of the Holy Spirit. When I went to college to prepare for the ministry, I was in a conversation early in my freshman year in which the subject of the Holy Spirit came up. I must have referred to the Holy Spirit as "it," because at the end of that discussion, one man in the group asked me if I'd meet with him later in his dorm room. He was a graduate student in theology so I was honored at the invitation and I gladly accepted.

When I went to his room, I was amazed to find that the walls were lined entirely with books. I felt that I was in the presence of a true scholar. He handed me a Greek New Testament, and I have to say, I was dismayed. I admitted to him that I had been at the college only a couple of weeks and I scarcely knew more than a few words and phrases in Greek. That didn't deter him. He proceeded to go through the New Testament with me, one verse after another, teaching me that the Holy Spirit is not an "it" but a "He"—a person, a member of the holy Trinity. My entire perspective changed.

- *Have you had an experience with the person of the Holy Spirit?*

_____

_____

When you begin to see the Holy Spirit as a person—not as a power or an experience—you have a much different perspective on receiving or getting the Holy Spirit.

From where does our false understanding of the Holy Spirit as an "it" tend to arise? In many cases, from Acts 2 where we read about the coming of the Holy Spirit into the lives of the first Christians:

When the Day of Pentecost had fully come, they were all with one accord in one place. And suddenly there came a sound from heaven, as of a rushing mighty wind, and it filled the whole house where they were sitting. Then there appeared to them divided tongues, as of fire, and one sat upon each of them. And they were all filled with the Holy Spirit and began to speak with other tongues, as the Spirit gave them utterance (Acts 2:1–4).

People tend to confuse the sights and sounds present at the Holy Spirit's arrival with the Holy Spirit Himself. They read of a rushing windlike sound from heaven. They read of a mass of fire that seems to divide into tongues that touch each person. They read of the people speaking in languages they didn't learn with their minds. And they assume that the sound, the fire, and the unknown tongues are the Holy Spirit.

These are manifestations of the Spirit's coming to the church on the day of Pentecost shortly after Jesus' ascension. They are *not* the Holy Spirit Himself. The sound is *as* a rushing mighty wind. The glowing light seems *as* divided tongues of fire. The Holy Spirit is infinitely more than any single manifestation of His presence.

The Characteristics of a Person

What makes a person a person—as opposed to any of God's other creatures? The three foremost qualities of personhood are these:

1. *Knowledge*—an ability to know, understand, recognize, and have meaning
2. *Will*—an ability to make choices and decisions on the basis of what one chooses to do, not as an instinctual response to external stimuli
3. *Emotion*—an ability to feel, both to have and express feelings and to be aware of them

Let's take a look at Scriptures that reveal these qualities associated with the Holy Spirit.

We read about the *knowing* ability of the Holy Spirit: "For what man knows the things of a man except the spirit of the man which is in him? Even so no one knows the things of God except the Spirit of God" (1 Cor. 2:11).

And we read about the *will* of the Holy Spirit: "But one and the same Spirit works all these things, distributing to each one individually as He wills" (1 Cor. 12:11).

In Romans 15:30, we read about "the love of the Spirit," and in Ephesians 4:30, we read Paul's admonishment: "Do not grieve the Holy Spirit of God." We can't grieve Somebody who doesn't love us. Because the Holy Spirit has an emotional capacity, we can grieve Him. Yes, the Holy Spirit has *emotions*.

As you read through the verses below, note as part of your recording of insights that these are all the actions or functions of a person.

What the Word Says	What the Word Says to Me
And I will pray the Father, and He will give you another Helper, that He may abide with you forever (John 14:16).	_____ _____ _____ _____
The Helper, the Holy Spirit, whom the Father will send in My name, He will teach you all things, and bring to your remembrance all things that I said to you (John 14:26).	_____ _____ _____ _____ _____
When the Helper comes, whom I shall send to you from the Father, the Spirit of truth who proceeds from the Father, He will testify of Me (John 15:26).	_____ _____ _____ _____ _____
And when He has come, He will convict the world of sin, and of	_____ _____

righteousness, and of judgment _____
(John 16:8). _____

Helping, comforting, teaching, calling to remembrance, testifying, convicting—these are all actions of a person.

* *What new insights do you have into the nature of the Holy Spirit?*

_____

_____

The Holy Spirit Is Part of the Trinity

The Holy Spirit is the third member of the triune Godhead: God the Father, God the Son, and God the Holy Spirit. He is inseparable from the Father and the Son; He is of one nature, character, and identity with them. At the same time, He is a unique person; He has a specific identity and function in our lives, just as Jesus has a specific identity and function and the Father has a specific identity and function. The Holy Spirit is present anytime the Father and the Son are present, and they in turn, are present anytime the Holy Spirit is present.

The Holy Spirit was present at creation: "The earth was without form, and void; and darkness was on the face of the deep. And the Spirit of God was hovering over the face of the waters" (Gen. 1:2). And He was vital in the creation of humankind:

> Then God said, "Let Us make man in Our image, according to Our likeness; let them have dominion over the fish of the sea, over the birds of the air, and over the cattle, over all the earth and over every creeping thing that creeps on the earth." So God created man in His own image; in the image of God He created him; male and female He created them (Gen. 1:26–27).

Note the word *Our*. We have been created in the full image of God the Father, God the Son, and God the Holy Spirit.

Now what does it mean to be created in God's image? To be created in God's image means that He has given us His qualities of personhood: we have an ability to know things and remember them, we have an ability to feel emotions and to respond to life with a full range of feelings, and we have an ability to make choices and decisions, to solve problems, to have "dominion" or authority over creation. We also have God's ability to help, to teach, to testify, to call to remembrance, to give convincing, convicting arguments. God has created us with the full capacity to be people.

As part of our creation, God "breathed" Himself into us. He imparted the capacity for His very nature to us. We have the specific ability to know God, to sense God at work in us, and to respond to God. He made us with the capacity to be His children and to invite Him into our lives.

You may ask, "Are you saying that the Holy Spirit is the Spirit of God?" That's exactly what I'm saying. We are wise to refer to Him in just that way:

- The Holy Spirit of God almighty
- The Holy Spirit of Christ Jesus—the same Spirit who indwelled Christ
- The Holy Spirit who indwells us today

All are one and the same Holy Spirit! His role in the Trinity is to fill, to energize, to empower, to cause to act, to compel behavior, to produce qualities of character, to work in and through God's creation.

He is not the Creator, but there was and is no creation without Him. He is not the Father, but there is no understanding of our need for relationship or confirmation of our relationship with the Father without Him. He is not God almighty, but there is no expression of or conviction about God's will apart from Him.

He is not the Son, but there are no awareness of sin and no coming to a saving knowledge of Jesus Christ as Savior apart from

Him. He is not Jesus, but Jesus did not do anything apart from the Holy Spirit's empowerment.

The Holy Spirit is inseparable from Christ Jesus and from God the Father.

- *What new insights do you have into the nature of the Holy Spirit?*

_____

_____

The Holy Spirit Is the Promise of God to the Believer

The Holy Spirit has a unique relationship with believers. Let the verses of Scripture below speak to you directly and personally. Keep in mind that Paul is writing in both cases to people who have accepted Jesus Christ as their Savior and who are following Him as the Lord of their lives.

What the Word Says	What the Word Says to Me
In Him you also trusted, after you heard the word of truth, the gospel of your salvation; in whom also, having believed, you were sealed with the Holy Spirit of promise, who is the guarantee of our inheritance until the redemption of the purchased possession, to the praise of His glory (Eph. 1:13–14).	_____ _____ _____ _____ _____ _____ _____ _____ _____ _____
But you are not in the flesh but in the Spirit, if indeed the Spirit of God dwells in you. Now if	_____ _____ _____

anyone does not have the Spirit
of Christ, he is not His. And if
Christ is in you, the body is dead
because of sin, but the Spirit is
life because of righteousness. But
if the Spirit of Him who raised
Jesus from the dead dwells in
you, He who raised Christ from
the dead will also give life to your
mortal bodies through His Spirit
who dwells in you (Rom. 8:9–11).

These verses say plainly that if you have Christ, you have the Holy Spirit of God. He is the seal of your commitment to Jesus Christ. In other words, when you accept Jesus Christ as the substitutionary, sacrificial, all-sufficient atonement for your sins—as an act of your confession and will—the Holy Spirit automatically seals that decision before the Father in heaven. You belong to God forever. There is no unsealing of what the Holy Spirit seals, not by your actions or by the actions of any other person.

Conversely, if you do not have the Holy Spirit resident in you, as God's seal and guarantee on your life—in other words, as God's claim that you belong to Him—you haven't received Jesus Christ as your Savior.

Can you be a Christian and not have the Holy Spirit? No.

Some people ask, "Have you received the Holy Spirit since you became a Christian?"

The question they ask is an impossibility. You received the Holy Spirit *as part of your receiving Christ.* You can't receive just one part of the Trinity. When you became a Christian—when you confessed your sins and repented of them, when you asked for and received God's forgiveness—you received the Holy Spirit. The Spirit of God came and indwelled your spirit and claimed you as His own. He has put you into full relationship with the Father and the Son, because He is inseparable from the Father and the Son.

He now seeks to live His life—the same quality of life that Jesus Christ lived—in you and through you.

• *Have you accepted Jesus Christ as your Savior?*

_____

_____

The Promise to Every Believer

Jesus promised the Holy Spirit to His disciples, and that promise extends to us as His disciples today. Recall that Jesus said, "But the Helper, the Holy Spirit, whom the Father will send in My name, He will teach you all things" (John 14:26). Jesus said the Father *will* send the Spirit.

At the time of Jesus' ascension, He said to His disciples, "Behold, I send the Promise of My Father upon you; but tarry in the city of Jerusalem until you are endued with power from on high" (Luke 24:49). It was the promise that Jesus had made to them on the night of the Last Supper—the promise of the Holy Spirit's coming to them to help and comfort them in His absence.

In Acts 1:8, we find these additional words at the time of Jesus' ascension: "You shall receive power *when* the Holy Spirit has come upon you; and you shall be witnesses to Me in Jerusalem, and in all Judea and Samaria, and to the end of the earth" (emphasis added). There was no doubt in His mind that it would happen for those who desired to follow Him.

Read Peter's description of the events on the day of Pentecost:

> This Jesus God has raised up, of which we are all witnesses. Therefore being exalted to the right hand of God, and having received from the Father the promise of the Holy Spirit, He poured out this which you now see and hear (Acts 2:32–33).

Peter was saying, "We received the One who was promised. You witnessed the manifestation of His presence coming into our lives with your own eyes and ears."

The Holy Spirit is God's promise to you as His child today. If you are a believer and follower of the Lord Jesus Christ, you have the Holy Spirit resident in you.

The Holy Spirit Is the Power of the Believer

Why did Jesus promise the Holy Spirit to those who followed Him? Because He knew that they would need to have the Holy Spirit in them if they were to be faithful, steadfast, and effective in their walk with God. The Holy Spirit enables people to live the Christian life.

What the Word Says

The God of our Lord Jesus Christ, the Father of glory, may give to you the spirit of wisdom and revelation in the knowledge of Him . . . that you may know . . . what is the exceeding great-ness of His power toward us who believe, according to the working of His mighty power which He worked in Christ when He raised Him from the dead and seated Him at His right hand in the heavenly places, far above all principality and power and might and dominion, and every name that is named, not only in this age but also in that which is to come. And He put all things under His feet, and gave Him to be head over all things to the church (Eph. 1:17–22).

What the Word Says to Me

_____
_____
_____
_____'.
_____
_____
_____
_____
_____
_____
_____
_____
_____
_____
_____
_____
_____
_____
_____
_____

Now to Him who is able to do ex-   _ _ _ _ _ _ _ _ _ _ _ _ _ _ _ _ _ _ _
ceedingly abundantly above all   _ _ _ _ _ _ _ _ _ _ _ _ _ _ _ _ _ _ _
that we ask or think, according   _ _ _ _ _ _ _ _ _ _ _ _ _ _ _ _ _ _ _
to the power that works in us, to   _ _ _ _ _ _ _ _ _ _ _ _ _ _ _ _ _ _ _
Him be glory in the church by   _ _ _ _ _ _ _ _ _ _ _ _ _ _ _ _ _ _ _
Christ Jesus to all generations,   _ _ _ _ _ _ _ _ _ _ _ _ _ _ _ _ _ _ _
forever and ever (Eph. 3:20).   _ _ _ _ _ _ _ _ _ _ _ _ _ _ _ _ _ _ _

Paul wanted the believers to know that they had full resurrection power in their lives. They had the same power that raised Christ Jesus from the dead. Certainly, such power was able to raise them from their sins. Not only that, but the power is above all other principality, power, dominion, or might. Nothing is more powerful than the Holy Spirit resident in you.

In our next lesson, we'll turn to what that power does in our lives.

- *How do you feel about the fact that if you are a believer in Christ Jesus, you have the power of the Holy Spirit in you?*

        —————————————————————————————

        —————————————————————————————

- *In what ways is the Lord challenging you in your spiritual walk with Him?*

        —————————————————————————————

        —————————————————————————————

LESSON 3

RELYING ON THE HOLY SPIRIT'S POWER IN US

The Holy Spirit's power in Christians is described by the Greek word *dunamis*. The same word gives rise to our English word *dynamite*. The Holy Spirit causes things to happen! His is an infinite power that blasts sin out of our lives.

What are the characteristics of the Holy Spirit's power in us? That's the question at the heart of this lesson.

The Holy Spirit Purifies Us

First and foremost, the power of the Holy Spirit purifies us. The nature of the Holy Spirit is often identified with fire. You will recall that the Holy Spirit's manifestation is described as "divided tongues, as of fire" (Acts 2:3).

Fire—or intense temperature—is used to melt and purify metals. This image appears in the Old Testament as applying to God's people: God will "thoroughly purge away your dross, and take away all your alloy" (Isa. 1:25). This same imagery can be applied to God's purification of the sinner of all that makes you impure before the Father. The Holy Spirit literally burns sin out of you so that you won't burn in your sin.

Recall that Paul wrote to the Romans: "If Christ is in you, the body is dead because of sin, but the Spirit is life because of righteousness. But if the Spirit of Him who raised Jesus from the dead dwells in you, He who raised Christ from the dead will also give life to your mortal bodies through His Spirit who dwells in you" (Rom. 8:10–11). The Holy Spirit not only burns sin from us, but He cleanses the fleshly nature so that we no longer desire to sin. In other words, once He has purified us, part of the purification process is a desire in us to remain pure.

What the Word Says	What the Word Says to Me
The words of the LORD are pure words, Like silver tried in a furnace of earth, Purified seven times (Ps. 12:6).	_____ _____ _____ _____ _____
Looking for the blessed hope and glorious appearing of our great God and Savior Jesus Christ, who gave Himself for us, that He might redeem us from every lawless deed and purify for Himself His own special people (Titus 2:13–14).	_____ _____ _____ _____ _____ _____ _____ _____

Fire and burning are not necessarily comfortable images to us. Fire sounds painful, and sometimes the fire of the Holy Spirit at work in our lives *is* painful. His chastisement and admonishment often go against what we desire in the fleshly, human nature. But the results of His purification process are glorious! As the Lord purifies us, we are made acceptable in His sight and are made ready for use in His kingdom. Purification is a necessary part of our being sanctified, which is to be cleansed and set aside as holy in God's eyes.

Purity of heart cannot be separated from the power of the Holy Spirit. That's a vital concept for you to understand.

You are purified by the Holy Spirit, and you continue to walk in purity because of the Holy Spirit's presence and power in you. There is no way you can clean up your life apart from His enabling you to do so.

Many people attempt to clean up their lives by a change in their behavior. They start going to church, attending a Bible study, giving some of their money to God, reading their Bibles, saying their prayers. None of these actions drive sin from their lives. Only as they yield to the Holy Spirit can they truly be cleansed completely.

- *Have you ever had what you might consider to be a refining experience by the Holy Spirit?*

_____

_____

- *How did you feel as the Holy Spirit refined you as if you were fine metal—before, during, and after the refining process?*

_____

_____

The Role of Conviction in Purification

Before we seek to be cleansed of sin, we must first be convicted that we have sinned. That is part of the Holy Spirit's purification process in us.

Paul wrote about this to the Corinthians. He asked them, "Do you not know that you are the temple of God and that the Spirit of God dwells in you? If anyone defiles the temple of God, God will destroy him. For the temple of God is holy, which temple you are" (1 Cor. 3:16–17).

No believer in Christ Jesus would think of defacing or destroying a church building. We consider our churches to be sacred places. In like manner, Paul taught the Corinthians that their bodies were sacred places. They were indwelled by God's Holy Spirit, just as the temple of old was filled with God's Holy Spirit.

In other words, the Corinthians had no right to themselves any longer. They belonged to God. They were His possessions. And the Holy Spirit will not allow anything to coexist with Him in His temple that is not holy, pure, and righteous.

For that reason, the Holy Spirit convicts us continually when we sin. We may turn a deaf ear to His conviction for such a long period that it seems His conviction has been reduced to a whisper, but He will convict us of our sin until we face it, confess it, repent of it, are forgiven for it, and are cleansed of it. Our sin is a stain on our purity before God, and the Holy Spirit will not allow it to stand unchallenged.

Be sensitive to the convicting power of the Holy Spirit in your life. Respond to Him with a contrite and humble heart. Face your sin. Only then can you be forgiven of it and restored to the purity necessary for the Lord to use you as He desires to use you.

- *In what ways do you feel challenged today to be purified by the Holy Spirit?*

The Holy Spirit Strengthens Us

A second aspect of the Holy Spirit's power in us is to impart strength to us. Paul prayed for the Ephesians that the Lord "would grant you, according to the riches of His glory, to be strengthened with might through His Spirit in the inner man" (Eph. 3:16).

For a person to be made strong implies that the person is initially weak by nature or has been weakened by circumstance. That certainly is true for any of us who are honest with ourselves. We struggle in staying obedient to God's Word. We are fragile in our bodies, frail in our resolve, and failing in our courage. We are weak creatures apart from the Holy Spirit.

Paul admonished the Ephesians that they were to grow into

maturity in Christ "to the measure of the stature of the fullness of Christ; that we should no longer be children, tossed to and fro and carried about with every wind of doctrine, by the trickery of men, in the cunning craftiness of deceitful plotting" (Eph. 4:13–14). We are to *become* strong in Christ, and the only way we can do that is through the Holy Spirit.

Without the Holy Spirit, you are weak. With the Holy Spirit, you are strong, even to the point that you can "do all things through Christ" who strengthens you (Phil. 4:13).

The Spirit of Christ is the same Holy Spirit who is working in your life. You *can* do all things that God commands you and calls you to do. You *can* live a quality of life that is the same as that lived by Christ Jesus. You *can* live a life free of sin and bold in speech and action because you are empowered by the same Holy Spirit who empowered Jesus.

Paul encouraged the Corinthians along these lines by reciting for them a long list of troubles he had experienced and then concluding, "Therefore most gladly I will rather boast in my infirmities, that the power of Christ may rest upon me. . . . For when I am weak, then I am strong" (2 Cor. 12:9–10).

Paul knew the reality of the Holy Spirit's power in his life, strengthening him to withstand and to recover from all kinds of persecution, trial, dangers, perils, weariness, and physical deprivation, including hunger, thirst, cold, and nakedness. He knew the power of the Holy Spirit strengthening him in times when he was afflicted by a "thorn in the flesh." (See 2 Cor. 11:23—12:7.) He told the Corinthians that he had learned this truth from the Lord: "My grace is sufficient for you, for My strength is made perfect in weakness" (2 Cor. 12:9).

Paul was no stranger to hardship, but he was also no stranger to God's power working in him. He knew that the source of his strength was solely the Lord.

The Holy Spirit revives us and gives us strength when we are weakened by disease, injury, or natural calamity. The Holy Spirit enables us to endure pain and times of trouble, adversity, and trial. The Holy Spirit enables us to say no to temptation, strengthening us in our resolve to be obedient to what God has commanded or called us to do. The Holy Spirit enables us to endure "to the end" in faith (Matt. 24:13).

What the Word Says	What the Word Says to Me
The LORD is their strength, And He is the saving refuge of His anointed (Ps. 28:8).	_____ _____ _____
The LORD is the strength of my life; Of whom shall I be afraid? When the wicked came against me To eat up my flesh, My enemies and foes, They stumbled and fell. Though an army may encamp against me, My heart shall not fear; Though war may rise against me, In this I will be confident (Ps. 27:1–3).	_____ _____ _____ _____ _____ _____ _____ _____ _____ _____ _____ _____ _____

Victory Over the Enemy

Ultimately, we are made strong by the power of the Holy Spirit so that we might defeat the devil. We are empowered against his

- *temptations.* The Holy Spirit helps us to resist impulses to sin against God and others (1 Cor. 10:12–13).
- *lies.* The Holy Spirit, as the Spirit of truth, helps us discern truth from lie and see the ploy of the devil against us (John 16:13).
- *attacks.* The Holy Spirit is part of our defensive armor against the enemy's assault (Eph. 6:18).

We are strengthened to resist the devil and in resisting him, to defeat his influence in our lives. (See James 4:7.) The devil seeks to accuse us before the Father at every turn of the road in our lives, but God's promise is that in our receiving Jesus Christ as our Savior, we have the strength of the Holy Spirit to withstand any of the devil's activity against us and thus, make his accusations null and void. (See Rev. 12:10.)

The Holy Spirit is omnipotent. He has all the power you can ever need or use—and infinitely more. Ask the Holy Spirit to impart the strength you need today.

What the Word Says	What the Word Says to Me
Then I heard a loud voice saying in heaven, "Now salvation, and strength, and the kingdom of our God, and the power of His Christ have come, for the accuser of our brethren, who accused them before our God day and night, has been cast down" (Rev. 12:10).	_____ _____ _____ _____ _____ _____ _____ _____
That He would grant you, according to the riches of His glory, to be strengthened with might through His Spirit in the inner man (Eph. 3:16).	_____ _____ _____ _____ _____

- *Have you ever had a strengthening experience in the Holy Spirit?*

  _____

  _____

- *How did you feel as the Lord strengthened you— before, during, and after His strengthening process?*

  _____

  _____

- *In what ways do you feel challenged today to ask the Holy Spirit to strengthen you?*

_____

_____

The Holy Spirit Equips Us for Ministry

Why does the Holy Spirit purify us and strengthen us? So God can use us! The Holy Spirit does His work *in* us, so He can do His work *through* us.

We are not indwelled by the Holy Spirit so that we can have an ecstatic experience or feel great joy or peace in our relationship with God. The emotions may arise as we experience the presence of the Holy Spirit at work in us. But the Holy Spirit indwells us so that we might be His witnesses and do His work on this earth.

Recall the words of Acts 1:8: "You shall receive power when the Holy Spirit has come upon you; and you shall be witnesses to Me in Jerusalem, and in all Judea and Samaria, and to the end of the earth."

The foremost manifestation of the Lord's presence in our lives is that we are His witnesses. We have changed lives that say something to the world in which we live. We speak with our very lives the gospel of Jesus Christ. We display by our words and deeds the power of God to transform people from a state of sinfulness to a state of righteousness. We are purified and strengthened so we might be living vessels of God's love and power made known to others.

In other lessons we will discuss in more depth the various types of equipping that the Lord does in our lives, but let it suffice at this point that you recognize this profound truth of God's Word: God wants to use *you*. He has a plan and a purpose for your life. He has a role for you to fill that only you can fill. If you are to accomplish the reason for your existence, to fulfill your destiny, and to know the inner satisfaction of a mission accomplished, you must have the power of the Holy Spirit at work in you.

We cannot succeed in God's eyes—with success that is eternally rewarding and abundantly enriching—apart from the Holy Spirit's help. We try to do so repeatedly in our lives, and each time we fall short. Anything that we try to do apart from the Holy Spirit's help and guidance is doomed to failure. It won't last. It can't. It has nothing of His eternal presence in it.

On the other hand, everything that we do in the Holy Spirit cannot help being eternal, life-giving, and a blessing to us and others.

In Him, we are and have all that is necessary forever. Without Him, we are and have nothing.

What the Word Says	What the Word Says to Me
I became a minister according to the gift of the grace of God given to me by the effective working of His power (Eph. 3:7).	_____ _____ _____ _____
In Him we live and move and have our being (Acts 17:28).	_____ _____
He who calls you is faithful, who also will do it (1 Thess. 5:24).	_____ _____

His Example Is Our Challenge

We noted in an earlier lesson that the Holy Spirit functions as helper, teacher, guide. All that the Holy Spirit is, He makes available to us so that we might, in turn, help, teach, guide, speak words of conviction, call God's truth to the remembrance of others.

The Holy Spirit has all knowledge. He gives us His wisdom so that we might make good decisions and sound judgments.

The Holy Spirit has capacity for all emotion. He imparts to us His great heart so that we might love others with an expanded ability.

The Holy Spirit operates out of His will. He imparts to us a knowledge of His will so that we might move in strength and obedience, and avoid the pitfalls of sin.

Ask the Holy Spirit today how He desires you to give testimony to His presence in your life and in what areas you need to let His witness shine brighter through you. What He calls you to do, He also equips you to do.

- *Have you ever had an equipping experience with the Holy Spirit?*

  _____

  _____

- *How did you feel as the Lord equipped you for service—before, during, and after?*

  _____

  _____

- *In what ways do you desire to be equipped by the Lord today? Or in what ways is the Lord challenging you today to become outfitted for greater ministry?*

  _____

  _____

LESSON 4

RELYING ON THE HOLY SPIRIT'S ABIDING PRESENCE

Has anyone ever asked you, "How many times have you been filled with the Holy Spirit?" Sometimes people speak in terms of an infilling of the Holy Spirit and then a refilling of the Holy Spirit in a person's life.

Let me assure you of this truth based on God's Word: when the Holy Spirit indwells you, He abides with you forever. He does not come and go. He is with you, from now into eternity.

Jesus had an encounter with a Samaritan woman at the well near the town of Sychar. Jesus asked her to give Him a drink from the well. She was puzzled that a Jew would ask a Samaritan for a drink, and He replied, "If you knew the gift of God, and who it is who says to you, 'Give Me a drink,' you would have asked Him, and He would have given you living water." She questioned the nature of the living water and Jesus said, "Whoever drinks of this water will thirst again, but whoever drinks of the water that I shall give him will never thirst. But the water that I shall give him will become in him a fountain of water springing up into everlasting life." (See John 4:1–14.)

At the last day of a feast in Jerusalem, Jesus said to an assembled multitude, "If anyone thirsts, let him come to Me and drink. He who believes in Me, as the Scripture has said, out of his heart will flow rivers of living water." John made it clear that Jesus was referring to the Holy Spirit as living water. He wrote, "But this He spoke concerning the Spirit, whom those believing in Him would receive; for the Holy Spirit was not yet given, because Jesus was not yet glorified." (See John 7:37–39.)

Living water refers to artesian springs—water that bubbles up through the rock formations of the earth in unending supply. The water from artesian springs is considered the purest, finest water available to humankind. It flows freely without end. This is the description Jesus chooses for the Holy Spirit that He will give to His followers—a freely flowing, unending inner source of purity, strength, power, and refreshment.

- *What new insights do you have from these two passages into the nature of the Holy Spirit?*

_____

_____

Not Yet Given?

John said that when Jesus spoke at the feast, the Holy Spirit "was not yet given, because Jesus was not yet glorified" (John 7:39). What does that mean?

Turn to John 14:15–18:

> If you love Me, keep My commandments. And I will pray the Father, and He will give you another Helper, that He may abide with you forever—the Spirit of truth, whom the world cannot receive, because it neither sees Him nor knows Him; but you know Him, for He dwells with you and will be in you. I will not leave you orphans; I will come to you.

Jesus is promising to send the very Spirit of God that indwells Him to His disciples to comfort them and help them. He makes it plain that His disciples will recognize the Holy Spirit because they have known Him as He has been manifested in Jesus. Furthermore, He says that the Holy Spirit will not be *with* them, which is the way they have experienced the Holy Spirit in the life of Jesus Christ. The Holy Spirit will be *in* them.

Jesus then repeats His command that they keep His word and explains further, "If anyone loves Me, he will keep My word; and My Father will love him, and We will come to him and make Our home with him" (John 14:23). Again, we see that the Holy Spirit who indwelled and worked through Jesus is the same Holy Spirit who is made available to us today as followers of Jesus.

Jesus tells His disciples that the "Helper, the Holy Spirit, whom the Father will send in My name, He will teach you all things, and bring to your remembrance all things that I said to you" (John 14:26), and He proceeds to command His disciples to abide in Him and to bear fruit. (See John 15:1–10.) He warns His disciples of persecution that will come and repeats His desire that they love one another. He says,

> But when the Helper comes, whom I shall send to you from the Father, the Spirit of truth who proceeds from the Father, He will testify of Me. And you also will bear witness, because you have been with Me from the beginning (John 15:26–27).

Again, we see that the Holy Spirit comes from the Father, but at the request of Jesus. The Holy Spirit will testify, Jesus says, about what Jesus is about to do on the cross—in other words, about His becoming our substitutionary, sacrificial, all-sufficient atonement for sin.

Jesus says He is telling His disciples all these things so that they won't stumble. Then He says,

> It is to your advantage that I go away; for if I do not go away, the Helper will not come to you; but if I depart, I will send

Him to you. And when He has come, He will convict the world of sin, and of righteousness, and of judgment: of sin, because they do not believe in Me; of righteousness, because I go to My Father and you see Me no more; of judgment, because the ruler of this world is judged. . . . He, the Spirit of truth . . . will guide you into all truth; for He will not speak on His own authority, but whatever He hears He will speak; and He will tell you things to come. He will glorify Me, for He will take of what is Mine and declare it to you (John 16:7–14).

The disciples are puzzled, of course, about how it can be more advantageous for Jesus to be away from them than for Him to be with them. Jesus, knowing their thoughts, says,

And in that day you will ask Me nothing. . . . Whatever you ask the Father in My name He will give you. Until now you have asked nothing in My name. Ask, and you will receive, that your joy may be full (John 16:23–24).

Up to now, the disciples have turned to Jesus for everything. They have trusted the Holy Spirit to work in Jesus to meet their needs and to deliver the people. After His death, resurrection, and ascension, the disciples no longer will have Jesus present with them in bodily form. But they will have the Holy Spirit inside them, they will be able to ask the Father in Jesus' name to meet their needs, and the Holy Spirit will work through them directly. That's why Jesus' going away is to their advantage. They will have the unlimited Holy Spirit of Christ available to them.

Until Jesus is crucified and resurrected, however, this will not happen. Until Jesus has gone away, He cannot send the Holy Spirit to His disciples.

As Jesus is about to ascend to His Father, He gathers His disciples together for one last word. We read, "He commanded them not to depart from Jerusalem, but to wait for the Promise of the Father, 'which,' He said, 'you have heard from Me; for John truly baptized with water, but you shall be baptized with the Holy Spirit not many days from now'" (Acts 1:4–5).

To recap what these Scriptures tell us: Jesus promises that the Holy Spirit will come *after* He has been glorified (through His death, resurrection, and ascension). He says that the Holy Spirit will be *in* His disciples. And He says that the Holy Spirit will be in them as living water, a continually available source of divine assistance. Jesus says nothing of the Spirit departing from His disciples at any time.

- *What new insights do you have into the nature of the Holy Spirit?*

  _____

  _____

- *How do you feel about the fact that the Holy Spirit comes to stay in the believer?*

  _____

  _____

This certainly must have been good news to the disciples, but it was also awesome news that they had difficulty understanding. Until that time, the Holy Spirit had not come to stay in the lives of men and women. That was not the pattern in the Old Testament.

The Holy Spirit's Presence in the Old Testament

In the Old Testament, we have repeated mention of the Holy Spirit and His empowerment of people to perform certain tasks. But there is a major difference between the operation of the Holy Spirit in the Old Testament and what Jesus promised to His disciples. The Holy Spirit came to individuals in the Old Testament to help them with specific works or ministries, and then He departed from them.

What the Word Says

What the Word Says to Me

Then the LORD spoke to Moses, saying: "See, I have called by name Bezalel the son of Uri, the son of Hur, of the tribe of Judah. And I have filled him with the Spirit of God, in wisdom, in understanding, in knowledge, and in all manner of workmanship, to design artistic works, to work in gold, in silver, in bronze, in cutting jewels for setting, in carving wood, and to work in all manner of workmanship" (Ex. 31:1–5).

So the LORD said to Moses: "Gather to Me seventy men of the elders of Israel, whom you know to be the elders of the people and officers over them; bring them to the tabernacle of meeting, that they may stand there with you. Then I will come down and talk with you there. I will take of the Spirit that is upon you and will put the same upon them; and they shall bear the burden of the people with you, that you may not bear it yourself alone" (Num. 11:16–17).

So the woman bore a son and called his name Samson; and the

child grew, and the LORD blessed
him. And the Spirit of the LORD
began to move upon him (Judg.
13:24–25).

Then Samuel took the horn of oil
and anointed him in the midst of
his brothers; and the Spirit of the
LORD came upon David from
that day forward (1 Sam. 16:13).

In each instance, the Spirit of the Lord comes upon these people to help them fulfill leadership roles—to help them carry out God's plan and purpose among His people. Even so, He helps in a wide variety of ways—artisans, judges, warriors, kings.

In other instances in the Old Testament, the Spirit comes upon people so that they may prophesy or speak in the name of the Lord. In Isaiah 61:1, we read,

> *The Spirit of the Lord GOD is upon Me,*
> *Because the LORD has anointed Me*
> *To preach good tidings to the poor.*

Ezekiel speaks about an indwelling of the Spirit to allow him to prophesy: "And He said to me, 'Son of man, stand on your feet, and I will speak to you.' Then the Spirit entered me when He spoke to me, and set me on my feet; and I heard Him who spoke to me" (Ezek. 2:1–2).

Now, the Holy Spirit does not work in the Old Testament in a manner contradictory to the manner in which He works in the New Testament. Certainly, the Holy Spirit works in the New Testament by providing leadership assistance and also by giving clear words of direction and truth. The difference is this: the Spirit does not abide continually with the people in the Old Testament.

This is evident in the life of Saul, whom Samuel anointed to be the first king of Israel. After David was anointed king, "the Spirit of the LORD departed from Saul" (1 Sam. 16:14).

The masses of people had no experience with the presence of the Holy Spirit. And we have no mention in the Old Testament of His coming to all the children of Israel at any time.

- *What is your emotional response to the fact that the Holy Spirit only rested on or indwelled certain people in the Old Testament, and that His presence was not permanent in their lives?*

_____

_____

The Holy Spirit in the Life of Jesus

In the Gospels are several instances in which the Holy Spirit is at work in the lives of individuals. Elizabeth had an experience with the Holy Spirit when Mary came to her house and she heard Mary's greeting. Elizabeth's baby, John the Baptist, leaped in her womb, and Elizabeth "was filled with the Holy Spirit." She then prophesied to Mary, "Blessed are you among women, and blessed is the fruit of your womb!" (See Luke 1:41–42.)

Zacharias, Elizabeth's husband, was struck speechless for doubting that Elizabeth might conceive John the Baptist in her old age. After Zacharias declared that their baby's name was to be John, "Zacharias was filled with the Holy Spirit," and he then prophesied about the ministry that his son would have as the "prophet of the Highest." (See Luke 1:67–79.)

We read also in Luke that "there was a man in Jerusalem whose name was Simeon, and this man was just and devout, waiting for the Consolation of Israel, and the Holy Spirit was upon him. And it had been revealed to him by the Holy Spirit that he would not see death before he had seen the Lord's Christ." Furthermore, Simeon was directed to go to the temple "by the Spirit" as Jesus' parents brought Him to the temple. Simeon declared that Jesus was the long-awaited Messiah. (See Luke 2:25–32.)

Each person experienced a short-lived experience with the Holy Spirit, and the purpose appeared to be to proclaim the work of the Lord as it related ultimately to the life and ministry of Jesus.

But what about the Holy Spirit in the life of Jesus Himself? We have a different picture from that of the Holy Spirit at work prior to Jesus' life.

First and foremost, Jesus was conceived by the Holy Spirit. The angel Gabriel told Mary, "The Holy Spirit will come upon you, and the power of the Highest will overshadow you; therefore, also, that Holy One who is to be born will be called the Son of God" (Luke 1:35).

Every moment of Jesus' earthly existence was filled with the Holy Spirit. He was conceived by the Holy Spirit and had the Holy Spirit residing in Him continually from that moment onward.

As Mary's son, Jesus was human in every way. As God's Son, Jesus was divine in every way. In coming to earth, Jesus gave up the glory that He had as God the Son in heaven, but He did not give up His divinity.

What Happened at Jesus' Baptism in Water?

Many people erroneously conclude that Jesus received the Holy Spirit into His life at His baptism in water by John the Baptist. Read what Matthew has to say about this:

> When He had been baptized, Jesus came up immediately from the water; and behold, the heavens were opened to Him, and He saw the Spirit of God descending like a dove and alighting upon Him. And suddenly a voice came from heaven, saying, "This is My beloved Son, in whom I am well pleased" (3:16–17).

Jesus obeyed the Father in being baptized by John, and in the aftermath, the Father revealed to Jesus in a special way that His earthly ministry was to begin. The manifestation by the Spirit was one of approval and of commissioning. The Spirit lighted "upon" Jesus, just as if the Father was tapping Him on the shoulder (as a king taps a knight on his shoulder with a sword). The Father declared His approval of Jesus and of the timing for His ministry to begin.

Nowhere in the Gospels do we have an account of Jesus receiving the gift of the Spirit or of His having an ecstatic or mystical experience with the Spirit. We have no mention that He grew in the Holy Spirit. We know that He "increased in wisdom and stature, and in favor with God and men" (Luke 2:52). All that refers to Jesus' growth in His humanity, not His divinity.

Jesus was fully God from His birth, even as He was fully man. He had no need to be filled with the Spirit, since He was always filled with the Spirit. He would not have been the Son of God otherwise.

What Happened in the Wilderness?

Immediately after Jesus was baptized, the Spirit led Him into the wilderness where He was tempted by Satan. Jesus withstood the temptation completely. His human will was tested, and it emerged 100 percent in alignment with the Spirit of God. The will of Jesus and the will of the Spirit were as one.

Jesus "returned in the power of the Spirit to Galilee" after His wilderness experience. (See Luke 4:14.) This does not mean that Jesus acquired the Holy Spirit in the wilderness or that He grew in the Holy Spirit while there. Jesus, "being filled with the Holy Spirit, returned from the Jordan and was led by the Spirit into the wilderness" (Luke 4:1). Jesus was already filled to complete fullness before He entered the time of temptation.

Jesus was not diminished in any way by the encounter with the devil during those forty days and nights. The devil gave Jesus his best shots, and Jesus rebuffed every one. There was no one moment in which Jesus was operating in anything less than the full power of the Holy Spirit.

Did Jesus Give Up the Spirit on the Cross?

No, He gave up His earthly sinless life as a sacrifice for our sins. He died *as* the Son of God.

We have no mention in the Scriptures that Jesus lost or gave up the Holy Spirit upon His crucifixion, at the time of His resurrection, or at the time of His ascension to the Father. He is filled with the Holy Spirit always. There has never been a moment throughout the ages when it has been otherwise. This permanent, unchanging presence of the Holy Spirit in Jesus' life qualifies Him as a member of the holy Trinity.

Jesus said repeatedly to His disciples that He didn't do anything that He didn't see the Father doing (John 5:19); He and the Father were one (John 10:30); and He knew the Father just as the Father knew Him (John 10:15). Jesus' entire ministry was marked by the fullness of the Holy Spirit.

The Holy Spirit and the Birth of the Church

So what happened on the day of Pentecost? Jesus sent His own Spirit, the Holy Spirit, to infill His church—His body of believers—just as His earthly physical body had once been filled. All believers in Christ are now His body:

> For as the body is one and has many members, but all the members of that one body, being many, are one body, so also is Christ. For by one Spirit we were all baptized into one body—whether Jews or Greeks, whether slaves or free—and have all been made to drink into one Spirit (1 Cor. 12:12–13).

On the day of Pentecost (*Pentecost* literally means the fiftieth day after the Passover feast), the Father extended the same Holy Spirit that resided in Jesus to infill all who believed and accepted what Jesus did on the cross. He sealed their redemption in so doing. (See Eph. 1:13.)

The glorious event of the Holy Spirit coming to Jesus' disciples marks the birthday of the church. It is the beginning of a new and lasting manifestation of the Holy Spirit.

The Holy Spirit in us is the life of Christ in us. It is His Spirit, in His body (ours individually and ours collectively as we are connected to other believers). And just as the Holy Spirit never departed from the life of Christ Jesus, so the Holy Spirit never departs from us. What a marvelous blessing He has made available to us—a blessing unknown by all who lived prior to the Cross!

- *What is your emotional response to the fact that the Holy Spirit abides with us always and never leaves us?*

Why Don't We Feel His Presence Always?

You may say, "If the Holy Spirit doesn't depart from me, why don't I always feel His presence?" There are many reasons. Sin limits the work of the Holy Spirit within you. The Lord may be chastising you or disciplining you in a certain way, and you may not feel the approval of the Holy Spirit until you conform to God's will for you. At times you may be too caught up in your activities and schedule to spend time with the Holy Spirit.

None of these circumstances are an indication that the Spirit has departed from you. On the contrary, if there has been any "departing," it is your own doing.

Feelings rise and fall. Feelings come and go. The Spirit does not. In other words, we may feel the Spirit in one time and place, and not in another time and place—not because of who He is in us, but because of the capricious nature of our human emotions.

And finally, the Holy Spirit grants special endowments of His presence and power at certain times. There are anointings associated with some ministry tasks and responsibilities. There are times when the Holy Spirit chooses to reveal Himself to us in powerful ways to encourage us, give us boldness, or cause us to take a specific action. This does not mean that the Holy Spirit comes and goes from us; rather, we more readily or more powerfully experience His presence and power in us at certain times.

You are sealed as Christ's own forever by the Holy Spirit the moment you confess your sins and receive the Father's forgiveness. It's up to you to abide in His presence, for He certainly is abiding in you.

What the Word Says	What the Word Says to Me
Then Peter said to them, "Repent, and let every one of you be baptized in the name of Jesus	_____ _____ _____

Christ for the remission of sins; and you shall receive the gift of the Holy Spirit. For the promise is to you and to your children, and to all who are afar off, as many as the Lord our God will call" (Acts 2:38–39).

While Peter was still speaking these words, the Holy Spirit fell upon all those who heard the word. And those of the circumcision who believed were astonished, as many as came with Peter, because the gift of the Holy Spirit had been poured out on the Gentiles also. For they heard them speak with tongues and magnify God. Then Peter answered, "Can anyone forbid water, that these should not be baptized who have received the Holy Spirit just as we have?" And he commanded them to be baptized in the name of the Lord (Acts 10:44–48).

- *Have you received the Holy Spirit into your life? Do you have an abiding awareness of the Holy Spirit's presence with you?*

- *What new insights do you have into the nature of the Holy Spirit and His relationship with you?*

- *In what ways do you feel the Lord challenging you in your spiritual walk today?*

RELYING ON THE HOLY SPIRIT IN PRAYER

Do you struggle in prayer? If you do, you aren't alone. Every Christian I know struggles at times in prayer, wondering, How should I pray about this situation or for this person? What is the Father's will in this instance? How should I express myself to the Father to convey what I really mean?

At times, our emotions run too deep for words, and we are therefore at a loss for words in prayer. At other times, we are confused by what we see as conflicting possibilities or problems. At still other times, we feel under such heavy assault from the devil that we seem to be fighting for our very lives, and all we can voice is a desperate cry for help!

Have you ever stopped to recognize that Jesus, in His humanity, struggled with prayer? Jesus knew that He had come to the earth to be the substitutionary, sacrificial, all-sufficient atonement for sin. He said to His disciples during the final week of His life,

The hour has come that the Son of Man should be glorified. Most assuredly, I say to you, unless a grain of wheat falls into the ground and dies, it remains alone; but if it dies, it produces much grain. . . . Now My soul is troubled, and what shall I say? "Father, save Me from this hour"? But for this purpose I came to this hour. "Father, glorify Your name" (John 12:23–24, 27–28).

Even with this knowledge and resolve, Jesus struggled. Matthew tells us that in the final hours before His betrayal by Judas, Jesus agonized in prayer in the Garden of Gethsemane. He admitted to His disciples, "My soul is exceedingly sorrowful, even to death. Stay here and watch with Me." Jesus prayed that if at all possible, He might be spared His crucifixion. Yet His ultimate prayer was, "O My Father, if this cup cannot pass away from Me unless I drink it, Your will be done." (See Matt. 26:37–42.) Luke adds that Jesus was in such agony as He prayed that "His sweat became like great drops of blood falling down to the ground" (Luke 22:44).

Yes, Jesus struggled with prayer. So do we if prayer means anything at all to us and if we feel a burden to intercede for others. And yet, in those times of struggle, the apostle Paul taught, we can take heart because "The Spirit also helps in our weaknesses. For we do not know what we should pray for as we ought, but the Spirit Himself makes intercession for us with groanings which cannot be uttered" (Rom. 8:26).

The Holy Spirit dwells within us to help us in our prayer lives! We can count on Him to make our prayers effective.

- *Have you struggled with prayer? Recall a particular incident. How did your struggle end?*

As We Pray

Jesus said that He would send a Helper to us—One who would be with us, in us, and upon us. He guides our prayers in very specific ways *as we pray*—by teaching us the meaning of God's Word and the words of Jesus as they apply to our particular situation, by reminding us of God's commandments and promises, by speaking to us of what Jesus did in His lifetime and through His death, by convicting us of sin, by guiding us into the way of righteousness before the Father, and by giving us the ability to judge right from wrong.

What the Word Says	What the Word Says to Me
I will pray the Father, and He will give you another Helper, that He may abide with you forever (John 14:16).	_____ _____ _____ _____
When the Helper comes, whom I shall send to you from the Father, the Spirit of truth who proceeds from the Father, He will testify of Me (John 15:26).	_____ _____ _____ _____ _____
And when He [the Helper] has come, He will convict the world of sin, and of righteousness, and of judgment (John 16:8).	_____ _____ _____ _____

Praying Within the Father's Will for Us

Our desire as Christians must always be to pray within the will of the Father for us. The Father's will includes all that is beneficial and good for us personally, and all that is beneficial and good for all His children—simultaneously and eternally.

His plan is greater than our ability to understand it; His purposes for our lives are beyond our comprehension. How, then, do we pray within the Father's will?

If we are praying for unsaved people, our prayer should be that they come to accept Jesus Christ as their personal Savior and then to follow Him as their Lord.

If we are praying for fellow believers in Christ Jesus, certain things are always within the will of the Father. We have a good model for this in Paul's letter to the Philippians, in which he tells the Philippians what he prays for them:

> I thank my God upon every remembrance of you, always in every prayer of mine making request for you all with joy, for your fellowship in the gospel from the first day until now, being confident of this very thing, that He who has begun a good work in you will complete it until the day of Jesus Christ.... And this I pray, that your love may abound still more and more in knowledge and all discernment, that you may approve the things that are excellent, that you may be sincere and without offense till the day of Christ, being filled with the fruits of righteousness which are by Jesus Christ, to the glory and praise of God (Phil. 1:3–6, 9–11).

We can pray these things for all believers at all times and in all situations:

- That Christ will complete the work in them that He has started
- That their love may abound
- That they may grow in knowledge and discernment
- That they may live sincere lives as they follow Christ, never bringing offense to His name
- That they may be filled with the fruits of righteousness
- That their lives may bring glory and praise to God

Colossians provides another model prayer that we can always pray for our fellow believers and know it is God's will:

> [We] do not cease to pray for you, and to ask that you may be filled with the knowledge of His will in all wisdom and

spiritual understanding; that you may walk worthy of the Lord, fully pleasing Him, being fruitful in every good work and increasing in the knowledge of God; strengthened with all might, according to His glorious power, for all patience and longsuffering with joy; giving thanks to the Father who has qualified us to be partakers of the inheritance of the saints in the light (Col. 1:9–12).

It is God's will always that our fellow believers know God's will, have God's wisdom, grow in spiritual understanding, walk in righteousness, bear fruit, grow in intimacy with the Lord, and be strong, patient, and joyful.

I encourage you to use these prayers as your basic pattern of intercession for others.

- *Have you ever had an experience in which you knew with certainty that you were praying in the Father's will for another person? Have you had an experience in which you felt your prayers were not what the Father desired?*

  _____

  _____

- *What new insights do you have into how to pray within the Father's will?*

  _____

  _____

When We Don't Know What to Pray or Can't Seem to Pray What We Desire to Pray

Our struggle with praying within the will of the Father occurs most often when we don't know how to pray or what to request. It may also occur when we do know how to pray, but the way we feel led to pray isn't the way others desire for us to pray.

Several years ago in my ministry, I visited a woman who was in the hospital. She was very ill, and she asked me to pray for her healing. I tried to pray as she requested, but the more I prayed, the more I prayed for everything but healing. In my spirit, I had a growing knowledge that healing was not God's plan for her. He was about to call her home. Sure enough, she died the next day.

In the difficult times when we don't know how to pray, or we find ourselves stopped from praying what we had intended to pray, Paul tells us the Holy Spirit "helps in our weaknesses" (Rom. 8:26). This phrase in Greek literally means that the Holy Spirit shares the load. He gets up under the burden that we feel—about our lives or others' lives—and He helps carry the prayer.

This same Greek word for help is used in Luke 10 where we read that Martha was distracted from sitting at Jesus' feet because she was concerned about getting a meal on the table. She asked Jesus to tell her sister, Mary, to help her in the serving preparations. (See Luke 10:40.)

The implication in both places is that the help being given or being sought is practical in nature. Martha is "cumbered about"—as the King James Version says—with serving her guests. This phrase implies that she was running in circles. That's the way we often feel in our prayers, isn't it? We run all around the problem, hoping to corral it.

We can trust the Holy Spirit to help us in a practical way—to guide us very specifically into God's answers and solutions so that we truly are praying in the will of the Father.

- *What new insights do you have into the role that the Holy Spirit plays in your prayer life?*

  _____

  _____

- *How do you feel about the fact that the Holy Spirit desires to help you pray?*

  _____

  _____

What Do We Have to Do to Receive the Help of the Holy Spirit?

We need to ask for it. Ask for His help before you pray. Ask for His help as you pray.

Don't Allow Yourself to Become Discouraged

At the very times you are most discouraged about prayer, don't give in to discouragement. That's the very time when you need to pray! Jesus promised that our Helper is always available and is instantly accessible. He is never out of the office when we need Him.

God values our prayers. Furthermore, He commands us to pray. Prayer is part of God's plan for accomplishing His purposes on this earth. We didn't design this plan for prayer. God did. And He intends for us to succeed in prayer. That's why He helps us in it.

The Holy Spirit Understands

The Holy Spirit understands fully everything you think, feel, or experience. Paul says that the Spirit both searches our hearts and knows the mind of the Father (Rom. 8:27). He sees with absolute clarity what we need and what the Father desires to give. The Holy Spirit understands three things simultaneously:

1. The situation we are facing. He sees its origins. He knows all the facets and all the details.

2. Our needs within the situation. Paul wrote to the Romans these words of encouragement: "What then shall we say to these things? If God is for us, who can be against us? He who did not spare His own Son, but delivered Him up for us all, how shall He not with Him also freely give us all things?" (Rom. 8:31–32).

God's plan is that we have everything we need to have so that we can do everything that He has called us to do.

3. The plan of God. First Corinthians 2:9–10 tells us,

> *Eye has not seen, nor ear heard,*
> *Nor have entered into the heart of man*
> *The things which God has prepared for*
> *those who love Him.*

But God has revealed them to us through His Spirit. For the Spirit searches all things, yes, the deep things of God.

As we pray, the Holy Spirit reveals the plan of God to us. How does this happen?

We pray for everything we know to pray for and about, and then we pause and listen for God to speak to us. We very likely won't hear Him speak with an audible voice, but suddenly, we think of additional things about which we might pray. We pray for these things, and then we listen again.

We continue this process, and we begin to receive a knowing from the Holy Spirit. We have a sense of resolution, of peace. We have deep assurance that God is answering us and that He is in control. At times, we may have clear direction—we know what to do, when to take action, and how to pursue God's answer.

We must receive this knowing by faith and thank the Lord for it, expressing not only our gratitude but also our intent to act on what the Lord has revealed to us. If we have misunderstood what the Lord has said to us, we can rest assured that He will be quick to correct us if we remain open to the leading and guiding of His Spirit.

Paul taught the Corinthians: "Now we have received, not the spirit of the world, but the Spirit who is from God, that we might know the things that have been freely given to us by God" (1 Cor. 2:12). As we pray—as we persist and persevere in prayer, refusing to end the prayer until we hear from God—we may also find that certain ideas or images or words come to our minds and hearts. They may be words of Scripture or of comfort or a message that has meaning to our specific situation. These things eventually form a pattern that is meaningful to us and represents God's answer to our need.

- *Have you had an experience in your prayer life in which you received a clear knowing in your spirit about what God desired for you to do?*

_____

_____

- *Have you had an experience in your prayer life in which you had a deep sense of peace and assurance that things were going to be all right, even if you did not have any specific direction or answer?*

Groanings of Intercession

Paul said that the Holy Spirit "makes intercession for us with groanings which cannot be uttered" (Rom. 8:26). The Holy Spirit does not carry our *words* of prayer to Jesus Christ, who in turn presents our petitions to the Father on the basis of His shed blood. Rather, the Holy Spirit carries the *meaning* of prayer to the Father. The Holy Spirit deals with us at the deepest levels of our being, and He knows what we truly need and desire. Regardless of what we may say with our lips, the Spirit knows what we mean in our hearts. He intercedes for us at that level, which is deeper than words.

The Holy Spirit then reveals to us the Father's response in ways that we understand, although we may not be able to express that response in words. We may have a knowing, deep within, that things are going to be all right, that an answer is on its way, that we can rest assured that the prayer has been heard and God is responding with compassion and love.

We should be encouraged because it means that we can never pray for the wrong thing. The Holy Spirit sees beyond our superficial understanding of our problem to the real issue that needs resolving. His answer to us is on the basis of our need and on God's plan. Therefore, His prayer for us and His answer to us are always in keeping with the will of the Father for us.

Intercessory Prayer for Others

Sometimes, we feel impressed to pray for people who are far away from us or for people we do not know. At other times, we can't seem to get a person's name off our minds, and we feel compelled to pray on the person's behalf.

If the Father knows all that is needed, and He knows His plan, what is the purpose in praying? The Father certainly can act without our prayers. The fact is, He hasn't chosen to do so. He invites our prayers, and He uses our prayers. When we intercede for others, our faith is built up in the process. We see how God has answered, and we grow in our confidence that God sees and cares about every detail of our lives.

- *Have you had an experience when you felt led by God to intercede for another person?*

  _____

  _____

- *How did you feel as you prayed—before, during, and after?*

  _____

  _____

- *What were the results? If you don't know the results, what do you believe God has done or will do?*

  _____

  _____

Is your prayer needed? Yes!

Is God listening? Yes!

Does God expect you to pray when He prompts you to pray? Yes!

Does God hear and answer your prayer? Yes!

Do you always pray for the right thing when you ask the Holy Spirit and rely on the Holy Spirit to join in your prayer with you? YES!

There is a great reward in cooperating with the Holy Spirit in prayer. That reward is manifested not only in the lives of those for whom you pray but also in your life.

What the Word Says	What the Word Says to Me
Whatever good anyone does, he will receive the same from the	_____ _____

Lord, whether he is a slave or
free (Eph. 6:8).

But you, beloved, building yourselves up on your most holy
faith, praying in the Holy Spirit,
keep yourselves in the love of
God, looking for the mercy of
our Lord Jesus Christ unto eternal life (Jude 20).

You can't lose if you ask the Holy Spirit to pray with you and
through you!

- *What new insights do you have regarding the Holy Spirit's help
  in your prayer life?*

  _____

  _____

- *How do you feel about the fact that you cannot fail in prayer
  when you ask for the Holy Spirit's help in your prayers?*

  _____

  _____

- *In what ways do you feel the Lord challenging you today?*

  _____

  _____

AVOIDING SIN AGAINST THE HOLY SPIRIT

Have you ever sinned against the Holy Spirit? Most people assume, and correctly so, that it is possible to sin against God the Father and against Jesus Christ, His Son. It is equally correct to assume that we sin against the Holy Spirit. In fact, all sins are against the Trinity. We sin against God.

The New Testament describes three specific ways, however, in which our actions are directly against the Holy Spirit: (1) quenching the Holy Spirit, (2) grieving the Holy Spirit, and (3) blaspheming against the Holy Spirit. When we do these things, we short-circuit His power in our lives. In this lesson we will take a look at each of these sins against the Holy Spirit and how we can avoid them in our Christian walk.

Quenching the Holy Spirit

Paul states very directly, "Do not quench the Spirit" (1 Thess. 5:19). As we discussed in an earlier lesson, fire has long been associated with the Holy Spirit. On the day of Pentecost, one of the manifestations of the Spirit was the appearance of "divided tongues, as of fire" resting on each person present. (See Acts 2:3.) Fire, in turn, is associated with cleansing, light, warmth, energy, refinement, and purifying.

Appropriately, the word *quench* means "to stifle or put out." Paul is saying, "Don't put out the fire of the Holy Spirit in your life. Don't throw cold water on the fire of God in your heart."

Now, we can never throw enough cold water on the fire of God to put out His fire completely in our lives. We cannot banish the Holy Spirit from our lives once we have confessed Christ. He has indwelled us and sealed our redemption.

But we can impede the effectiveness of the Holy Spirit working in our lives. We can override His will, reject His promptings, or ignore His presence with us.

Have you ever been in the room with another person who ignored you completely? We say that such a person gave you the cold shoulder. We can do that to the Holy Spirit in our lives.

And in so doing, we cut short the work that the Holy Spirit might otherwise do in us and through us. He will not move beyond our will or beyond our invitation or request to invite Him to work in us. His work in our lives is only as powerful and effective as we desire and allow it to be.

What the Word Says

Be strong in the Lord and in the power of His might (Eph. 6:10).

Praying always with all prayer and supplication in the Spirit, being watchful to this end with all perseverance and supplication for all the saints (Eph. 6:18).

May the God of all grace ...

What the Word Says to Me

_____

_____

_____

_____

_____

_____

_____

perfect, establish, strengthen, and settle you (1 Peter 5:10).

God's desire for us is that we be strong in the Holy Spirit—that we accept His full work in our lives and that we act boldly in the fullness of His power.

How Do We Quench the Spirit?

The foremost ways that we quench the work of the Holy Spirit are these:

We say no to something God directs us to do. We choose our will over His will. We choose to go our own way. The Holy Spirit can do nothing to help us and to keep us in the center of God's plan and purpose for our lives if we willfully turn away from His leading and choose to pursue our desires and goals. He will not help us do something that He knows is contrary to God's best for us.

We can ignore His presence. Again, this is a matter of the will. We can go about living our lives and refuse to acknowledge His help, invite His help, or accept His help.

We can sin repeatedly. Our sin causes the Holy Spirit to abandon any positive, forward-moving implementation for our blessing so that He might convict us of our sin. When we sin, we evoke the chastisement and chiding of the Holy Spirit in our lives. He cannot reward our unfaithfulness. He cannot participate in our rebellion. We quench His eager desire to produce good fruit in us, for us, and through us.

What Can We Do?

We can choose to keep our relationship with the Spirit kindled. Any person who has ever camped or had a wood-burning fireplace knows that it's easier to keep a fire burning than it is to build a fire. Maintain your ongoing relationship with the Holy Spirit. Talk to Him daily, just as you might pray to God the Father. Recognize His presence. Ask for His help. Invite Him to lead and guide you into right paths and right decisions.

When you sin, be quick to respond to His convicting nudges in your life. Confess your sin immediately, and repent of it, turning back to the way that you know God desires for you to walk.

When the Holy Spirit prompts you to move in a certain direction, say yes. Don't hesitate. Respond quickly to say what He compels you to say or do what He leads you to do. Choose to stay strong in the Lord.

- *In your Christian walk, have you ever had a time in which you recognized that you had quenched the Holy Spirit's work within you? How did you feel?*

_____

_____

- *In what ways is the Lord challenging you today?*

_____

_____

Grieving the Holy Spirit

A second way in which we limit or short-circuit the effective work of the Holy Spirit in our lives is through grieving the Holy Spirit. Paul wrote to the Ephesians, "Do not grieve the Holy Spirit of God, by whom you were sealed for the day of redemption" (Eph. 4:30).

This admonition is embedded within a passage in which Paul admonished the believers in Ephesus to "no longer walk as the rest of the Gentiles walk" but to "put on the new man which was created according to God, in true righteousness and holiness" (Eph. 4:17, 24). He told them to put away from their lives lying (v. 25), anger (v. 26), stealing (v. 28), and corrupt speech (v. 29).

He summed up his statement to them, "Let all bitterness, wrath, anger, clamor, and evil speaking be put away from you, with all malice. And be kind to one another, tenderhearted, forgiving one another, even as God in Christ forgave you" (vv. 31–32).

How do we grieve the Holy Spirit? We grieve Him when we disobey God's commandments and when we choose to act in unrighteous ways. In other words, we know what to do and then choose to do the opposite.

The Ephesians knew it was not godly to lie, steal, be angry with one another, or speak cutting, hurting words to one another. They knew that such things gave "place to the devil" (v. 27).

Paul lived and ministered among the Ephesians for two years, and his ministry had a powerful impact on the city of Ephesus. And yet, Paul had to remind the Christians not to do those things! It was as if he had to go back to square one with them. When the Ephesians broke the most obvious of God's commandments, they caused sorrow in the Holy Spirit. Paul said, "Your behavior breaks the heart of God."

The Holy Spirit is grieved because He loves us and He deeply desires to reward us, bless us, and see good fruit produced in and through us. He knows that sin destroys us and causes negative consequences in our lives. When we know that loved ones are doing something that will cause them harm, we are grieved. So is He.

How Can We Avoid Grieving the Holy Spirit?

We can choose to keep God's commandments and to lead a disciplined life. When we sin, we must confess the sin immediately and repent of it, changing our minds and our behavior to conform to God's statutes.

As we ask the Holy Spirit to lead us and help us on a daily basis, we have His help in our Christian walk. He keeps our footing sure. He gives us the courage to withstand temptation.

What the Word Says	What the Word Says to Me
And do not lead us into temptation, but deliver us from the evil one (Matt. 6:13).	_____ _____ _____
Your hands have made me and fashioned me; Give me understanding, that I may learn Your commandments (Ps. 119:73).	_____ _____ _____ _____

Take My yoke upon you and
learn from Me, for I am gentle
and lowly in heart, and you will
find rest for your souls (Matt.
11:29).

_____

_____

_____

_____

_____

- *Have you had an experience in your life in which you recognize that you grieved the Holy Spirit? How did you feel?*

- *In what ways is the Lord challenging you today?*

Blaspheming Against the Holy Spirit

In Matthew 12, we read about a confrontation between Jesus and the Pharisees, some of the religious leaders who were plotting to destroy Him because of the miracles that He had done on the Sabbath. Jesus knew what the Pharisees were up to, and what their real motivations were, but He continued His work among the people and healed a man who was demon-possessed and could not see or hear. There was no doubt that the man had been healed and delivered in a powerful way.

The Pharisees, intent solely on destroying the credibility of Jesus, insisted that Jesus had healed by the power of Beelzebub, the ruler of the demons. Jesus replied, "Every kingdom divided against itself is brought to desolation" (Matt. 12:25). In other words, Satan isn't going to empower or inspire anybody to do something that is good. Satan would be setting up his own down-fall.

The Pharisees were also making a statement about God—that God would not empower someone like Jesus to do good on the Sabbath. They were saying, in essence, God is content to let certain people starve or suffer on the Sabbath, and for certain people to remain demon-possessed, unable to see or hear. But the ruler of the demons, Beelzebub, is willing to see such people helped and healed. They had completely turned upside down the truth about God and the devil.

Jesus said to them, "He who is not with Me is against Me, and he who does not gather with Me scatters abroad" (Matt. 12:30). And then He added,

> Therefore I say to you, every sin and blasphemy will be forgiven men, but the blasphemy against the Spirit will not be forgiven men. Anyone who speaks a word against the Son of Man, it will be forgiven him; but whoever speaks against the Holy Spirit, it will not be forgiven him, either in this age or in the age to come (Matt. 12:31–32).

Jesus was saying, "You can say what you will about Me, but don't speak such perversion about the Spirit of God. When you blaspheme against God in that way, you are saying, in effect, that God does not desire to forgive and deliver people. And as long as you believe that and teach that to others, you won't be able to experience His forgiveness and deliverance. If you don't believe God wants to forgive people and restore people to wholeness, you will never be open to the sacrifice that I will make on the cross of Calvary."

Those words of Jesus were to the Pharisees, people who had put themselves into sharp conflict with Jesus and who were plotting His destruction. Those words were spoken to them before the death of Jesus on the cross and before His resurrection. Those words were spoken as a warning to the Pharisees to let them know that He knew the full intent of their hearts and the full meaning of their claims.

This sin of blaspheming against the Holy Spirit is called an unpardonable sin in this passage.

First, let me assure you that if you have any concern about having committed the unpardonable sin—any concern that you might not be right with God, even though you hope and desire to be right with God—there is no way you can have committed the unpardonable sin.

Second, this is the only time we find these words in the Scriptures and the message is solely to the Pharisees who were cutting themselves off from the possibility of acknowledging Jesus as their Savior and Lord. At no other time in the New Testament, however, do we find mention of an unpardonable sin. There are no warnings against it or teachings about it. To the contrary, numerous passages of Scripture announce that God's forgiveness is freely given and readily available for the asking.

What the Word Says	What the Word Says to Me
For God so loved the world that He gave His only begotten Son, that whoever believes in Him should not perish but have everlasting life (John 3:16).	_____ _____ _____ _____ _____
For the wages of sin is death, but the gift of God is eternal life in Christ Jesus our Lord (Rom. 6:23).	_____ _____ _____ _____
If we confess our sins, He is faithful and just to forgive us our sins and to cleanse us from all unrighteousness (1 John 1:9).	_____ _____ _____ _____

What we should be concerned about when it comes to blaspheming against the Spirit is not that the sin is pardonable or unpardonable, but that when we refuse to receive the forgiveness that God freely offers, we put ourselves into an unpardonable state. We can die in an unpardonable state, but it won't be because we have committed an unpardonable sin.

No sin is unforgivable on this side of death. It is equally true that no sin can be forgiven on the other side of the grave.

Refusing to believe in the forgiveness made available to us by the death of Christ brings about everlasting death. Accepting what Jesus did on the cross—believing in Him as Savior—brings about everlasting life.

In like manner, when we willfully turn away from God and pursue the lusts of the flesh and operate out of our pride, when we know that we need God's forgiveness but refuse to confess our sins and receive His forgiveness, we tie the hands of the Holy Spirit in our lives. He will not force us to experience God's will for us. He will convict us of our sin, speak to us of Jesus, and chastise us for our rebellion, but He will not override our choices.

Because you are a Christian, your rebellion will not put you into an unpardonable state, but it will put you into a miserable state! You cannot be happy or know the fullness of God's joy, peace, and blessings if you are in sin and refuse God's forgiveness. You will be cut off from the fullness of your potential and the maximum blessing that God has for you in achieving your destiny in Him. And you will remain in that miserable state until you confess your sins to God and receive His forgiveness.

- *Have you ever rebelled against God since you became a Christian? How did you feel?*

  _____

  _____

- *What new insights do you have into the nature and work of the Holy Spirit in our lives?*

  _____

  _____

- *In what ways are you feeling challenged in your spiritual walk?*

  _____

  _____

Relying on the Holy Spirit to Reproduce Christ's Character in Us

What would you answer if someone asked you, "How can you identify a Christian?" The Bible's answer is that a Christian will bear the fruit of the Holy Spirit—a Christian will display the same character qualities that Jesus Christ displayed during His life on this earth. Fruit is the outward expression that we are true followers of Jesus Christ.

The theme of fruit bearing is important in the ministry of Jesus. In the Sermon on the Mount, Jesus said,

> Beware of false prophets, who come to you in sheep's clothing, but inwardly they are ravenous wolves. You will know them by their fruits. Do men gather grapes from

thornbushes or figs from thistles? Even so, every good tree bears good fruit, but a bad tree bears bad fruit. A good tree cannot bear bad fruit, nor can a bad tree bear good fruit. Every tree that does not bear good fruit is cut down and thrown into the fire. Therefore by their fruits you will know them (Matt. 7:15–20).

What Jesus said in a negative reference to false prophets, He repeated in positive terms to His disciples:

I am the true vine, and My Father is the vinedresser. Every branch in Me that does not bear fruit He takes away; and every branch that bears fruit He prunes, that it may bear more fruit. . . . Abide in Me, and I in you. As the branch cannot bear fruit of itself, unless it abides in the vine, neither can you, unless you abide in Me. I am the vine, you are the branches. He who abides in Me, and I in him, bears much fruit; for without Me you can do nothing. If anyone does not abide in Me, he is cast out as a branch and is withered; and they gather them and throw them into the fire, and they are burned. If you abide in Me, and My words abide in you, you will ask what you desire, and it shall be done for you. By this My Father is glorified, that you bear much fruit; so you will be My disciples (John 15:1–2, 4–8).

Without a doubt, Jesus expects us to bear fruit in our lives—the fruit of His likeness.

What the Word Says

Not everyone who says to Me, "Lord, Lord," shall enter the kingdom of heaven, but he who does the will of My Father in heaven. Many will say to Me in that day, "Lord, Lord, have we not prophesied in Your name,

What the Word Says to Me

_____

_____

_____

_____

_____

_____

_____

cast out demons in Your name, and done many wonders in Your name?" And then I will declare to them, "I never knew you; depart from Me, you who practice lawlessness!" (Matt. 7:21–23).

You did not choose Me, but I chose you and appointed you that you should go and bear fruit, and that your fruit should remain, that whatever you ask the Father in My name He may give you (John 15:16).

Peter Was a Fruit Bearer

Peter is a great example of the Holy Spirit's working in a person's life to bear fruit. As an apostle of Jesus, Peter had followed Him closely for nearly three years. He had been a witness to His many miracles. He had heard His sermons. He had watched His life. Peter had even walked on water with Jesus! But in the aftermath of Jesus' arrest in the Garden of Gethsemane, Peter—whom Jesus had called a rock—denied three times that he knew his beloved Master.

But what happened after Peter received the Holy Spirit on the day of Pentecost? He preached one of the most powerful sermons in the Scriptures and said to the very ones to whom he hadn't dared open his mouth,

Men of Israel, hear these words: Jesus of Nazareth, a Man attested by God to you by miracles, wonders, and signs which God did through Him in your midst, as you yourselves also know—Him, being delivered by the determined purpose and foreknowledge of God, you have taken by lawless hands, have crucified, and put to death (Acts 2:22–23).

Those are not the words of a timid man. Those are words of bold proclamation.

Peter was bearing good fruit!

- *Have you had before-and-after experiences of courage since you received the Holy Spirit into your life?*

_____

_____

Two Types of Fruit

Two types of fruit are indicated in the teachings of the Scriptures. The first is the fruit of works and deeds. Jesus cites this type of fruit in Matthew 7. The false prophets are known by their evil words and deeds.

The second type of fruit is that of character. This inner fruit is the more important since what we do is always a natural overflow of who we are. We may be able to hide our bad character behind good deeds for a while, but eventually, our true character will display itself.

Galatians 5:19–23 describes the character traits that the Lord desires for us to have:

> Now the works of the flesh are evident, which are: adultery, fornication, uncleanness, lewdness, idolatry, sorcery, hatred, contentions, jealousies, outbursts of wrath, selfish ambitions, dissensions, heresies, envy, murders, drunkenness, revelries, and the like; of which I tell you beforehand, just as I also told you in time past, that those who practice such things will not inherit the kingdom of God. But the fruit of the Spirit is love, joy, peace, longsuffering, kindness, goodness, faithfulness, gentleness, self-control. Against such there is no law.

What the Word Says	**What the Word Says to Me**
Walk in the Spirit, and you shall not fulfill the lust of the flesh. For the flesh lusts against the Spirit, and the Spirit against the flesh; and these are contrary to one another, so that you do not do the things that you wish (Gal. 5:16–17).	_____ _____ _____ _____ _____ _____ _____ _____
But fornication and all uncleanness or covetousness, let it not even be named among you, as is fitting for saints; neither filthiness, nor foolish talking, nor coarse jesting, which are not fitting, but rather giving of thanks. For this you know, that no fornicator, unclean person, nor covetous man, who is an idolater, has any inheritance in the kingdom of Christ and God (Eph. 5:3–5).	_____ _____ _____ _____ _____ _____ _____ _____ _____ _____ _____

God's standard for fruit bearing is righteousness, purity, and obedience to God's moral law. Paul repeatedly warned the gentile Christians that there is no provision whatsoever in the gospel for impurity. There is no license to sin.

- *How do you feel about God's challenge to you to bear good fruit of both character and deeds? Which seems easier?*

  _____

  _____

- *In what ways is the Lord challenging you today?*

_____

_____

The Nature of Fruit Bearing

I want you to note some aspects of fruit bearing in the Scriptures.

First, we are commanded to bear fruit. This is not an option. The words of Jesus and the writers of the New Testament are in a command or imperative tense. *Abide* in Me. *Bear* fruit. *Walk* in the Spirit. *Make* the tree good.

Second, we are to bear good fruit. We have a choice in the type of fruit that we will produce, and both Jesus and Paul admonish us to bear fruit that is recognized as good by God, saint, and sinner alike.

Good fruit is beautiful to behold—it is almost irresistible. Good fruit is also sound; it isn't damaged by disease or bruising. Good fruit bears within it healthy seeds that produce new life. In spiritual terms, good fruit draws others to Christ and is not tainted by sin. Such fruit has within it something that will last forever or that will produce everlasting results. Only the work of the Holy Spirit is truly good, for only His work is eternal, completely without blemish, and compels others to accept Christ Jesus as their Savior.

Fruit that is produced by the Holy Spirit has the same quality of goodness that is found in the Spirit Himself. In Jesus' analogy of Himself as the vine, the Holy Spirit is the life force flowing through the vine and producing fruit within us. Since Jesus was indwelled by the same Holy Spirit who now indwells us, we produce the same good fruit in our lives that was manifested in Jesus' life.

The Holy Spirit is the source of any goodness in us. We may think we are good people, but apart from the Holy Spirit and the life of Christ He is producing in us, we are not good. Our pride causes us to think that we can produce goodness on our own.

Third, we are to bear much fruit. Our lives are to be overflowing with the fruit of the Spirit. From a character standpoint, our nature is to be overflowing with the goodness of Christ Jesus. Our love is to be abundant love, our joy is to be exuberant joy, our peace is to be all-encompassing peace, and so forth. We are to be continually at work in God's kingdom, doing whatever the Lord leads us to do to the best of our ability and with the maximum effort.

The fruit mentioned in Galatians 5:22 is singular—the "fruit" of the Spirit, not the "fruits" of the Spirit. When we receive the life of the Holy Spirit within us, we get all of the Holy Spirit. Thus, all of His traits become our traits. He doesn't award them to us bit by bit. We receive the full nature of the Holy Spirit.

The abundance of fruit that we manifest, however, is subject to the will. We can refuse to do what the Spirit prompts us to do.

- *What new insights do you have into the nature of the fruitfulness of the Holy Spirit in and through your life?*

_____

_____

What About the Unfruitful?

Jesus said that every branch that doesn't produce is taken away or, as some translations say, "cast away" (John 15:2). There are two possible interpretations for this phrase "cast away." One is to be lifted up off the ground. In the Middle East, the branches of vines are often left to grow close to the ground rather than trained on wires or trellises as they are in Europe and the United States. To "cast away" or "take away" a branch can mean to lift up the branch to train it along a stake or wire. To "cast away" can also mean to cut off and discard. In either case, the vine is moved or removed from its current position.

In the lives of unbelievers, these words should hold a stinging conviction. Those who don't abide in Christ are subject either to being lifted up (which can mean that they confess Christ and are saved and made fruitful) or to being removed by death. If they don't abide in Christ, they are subject to change—either positive or negative.

Some people try to act as if they are producing fruit. They go through the motions of attending church, doing church work, claiming to pray and read God's Word. They'll do their best to convince you that they are people of good character. But they aren't connected to the Vine. They have never been born again in the spirit. As a result, they do not receive the life-giving, fruit-bearing sustenance of the Holy Spirit. They have not been grafted into Christ. Eventually, their state is revealed. The branches wither and are cast away.

If you have any doubt about whether you are grafted into Christ Jesus, confess to God that you are a sinner, and ask for His forgiveness today. Receive what He freely offers to give you. Then repent of your old ways, and rely on the Holy Spirit to produce genuine fruit in your life.

If you are a believer and you are not producing much good fruit in your life, the Lord is not going to remove you from Himself. But He is going to continue to convict you of any sin in your life until you let it go, ask for forgiveness, and invite the Lord to cast your sin away from you. The Lord also says that those who are bearing fruit—although not necessarily much fruit—are subject to being pruned so they will bear more fruit.

Sin can stop the flow of the Spirit in our lives and result in dead wood in our souls. Our neglect of the things of God and of our relationship with God can cause dead wood. We can become so busy, and have our priorities so out of line, that the flow of the Spirit in us is thwarted and part of us seems to die out.

If any of these conditions apply to you today, confess that to the Lord, repent of your behavior, receive His forgiveness, and make a new start in your life. Choose to bear much fruit.

Invite the pruning work of the Holy Spirit into your life. Ask Him to show you in which areas you need to change your mind and your behavior.

- *In what ways is the Lord challenging you today in your spiritual walk with Him?*

_____

_____

The Pruning Process

Pruning can be painful. It can seem drastic at times. Early in my ministry, I pastored a church in Fruitland, North Carolina. One day I called on a member of our congregation who was in his apple orchard, pruning an apple tree. I was shocked at how severely he was pruning the tree, and I said to him, "You're going to _kill_ that tree." He looked at me with the eyes of many years of experience in pruning apple trees and said, "You stick to preaching and I'll do the pruning."

At times, you may feel as if God is killing you with the severity of His pruning, but be encouraged. He is getting ready for a great harvest of fruit in your life.

What the Word Says	What the Word Says to Me
It is no longer I who live, but Christ lives in me; and the life which I now live in the flesh I live by faith in the Son of God (Gal. 2:20).	_____ _____ _____ _____ _____
By this we know that we love the children of God, when we love God and keep His commandments. For this is the love of God, that we keep His commandments (1 John 5:2–3).	_____ _____ _____ _____ _____
[Jesus] bore our sins in His own body on the tree, that we, having	_____ _____

died to sins, might live for righteousness (1 Peter 2:24).

_____

_____

Live according to God in the
spirit (1 Peter 4:6).

_____

_____

- *Have you had a pruning experience with the Lord?*

  _____

  _____

- *How does it feel to be pruned—before, during, and after?*

  _____

  _____

- *In what ways is the Lord challenging you today to produce more good fruit?*

  _____

  _____

Fruit bearing was never intended to be difficult. A cluster of grapes doesn't have to work at becoming sweet or ripe. Neither do we. The fruit bearing in our lives is automatic if we remain in the Vine. Our job is to abide. His job is to produce fruit in us and through us. As long as we stay true to the Lord, walk in obedience to Him, and desire for Him to have control over our lives, the fruit in us grows naturally and according to His time schedule.

We can't force fruit to grow. We can only cling to Jesus and choose to follow the daily leading of the Holy Spirit in our lives. *Our heavenly Father* is the Vinedresser. *Jesus* is the Vine. The *Holy Spirit* is the life-giving force flowing through the Vine. We are the branches that bear His fruit.

- *What new insights do you have into the nature of the Holy Spirit and His work in your life?*

_____

_____

- *In what ways do you feel challenged in your spiritual walk?*

_____

_____

LESSON 8

RELYING ON THE HOLY SPIRIT FOR SPIRITUAL GIFTS

Do you feel inadequate in your ability to serve others? Do you feel incapable of ministry? Do you wish that your ministry to others might be more effective?

I have good news for you today! You are not alone in your ministry. The Holy Spirit within you will equip you for ministry and then will help you do it. The results are completely in His hands, and what the Holy Spirit does is always successful and effective. Paul wrote to the Thessalonians, "He who calls you is faithful, who also will do it" (1 Thess. 5:24).

"But," you may say, "I'm not sure that now is the right time for me to be part of a ministry to others or to take on any service to others."

Now is always the time in God's eyes. If you refuse to give of yourself to others, not only will you miss the blessing that comes from your giving on this earth, but you will miss a blessing in heaven. Of equal importance, you will be a hindrance to the work of God on this earth. The Lord is counting on you to minister to others, which means to serve others, give to others, help others. That's part of the life in Christ that He has ordained for you.

Many people think of ministry only in terms of full-time church work or work as a missionary or in a church-related organization. Ministry occurs anytime we do something in the name of Jesus for the benefit of others.

Jesus was very clear on this point:

> "I was hungry and you gave Me food; I was thirsty and you gave Me drink; I was a stranger and you took Me in; I was naked and you clothed Me; I was sick and you visited Me; I was in prison and you came to Me." Then the righteous will answer Him, saying, "Lord, when did we see You hungry and feed You, or thirsty and give You drink? When did we see You a stranger and take You in, or naked and clothe You? Or when did we see You sick, or in prison, and come to You?" And the King will answer and say to them, "Assuredly, I say to you, inasmuch as you did it to one of the least of these My brethren, you did it to Me" (Matt. 25:35–40).

The Lord expects us to be His ministers on this earth—to be His hands and feet. He describes those who follow Him as His body. We are to do collectively, under the direction of the Holy Spirit, what Jesus did in His earthly body—minister to others in healing, deliverance, and the preaching of good news. And because we are many in number, our ministry multiplies what Jesus did. We are to do what Jesus did. We are to be like Him in character, in thought, in word, and in deed.

- *How do you feel about the fact that you are to be like Jesus and do what Jesus did?*

_____

_____

What the Word Says	What the Word Says to Me
The LORD has anointed Me To preach good tidings to the	_____ _____

poor;
He has sent Me to heal the bro-
kenhearted,
To proclaim liberty to the
captives,
And the opening of the prison to
those who are bound;
To proclaim the acceptable year
of the LORD . . .
To give them beauty for ashes,
The oil of joy for mourning,
The garment of praise for the
spirit of heaviness (Isa. 61:1–3).

The cup of blessing which we
bless, is it not the communion of
the blood of Christ? The bread
which we break, is it not the communion of the body of Christ?
For we, though many, are one
bread and one body; for we all
partake of that one bread (1 Cor.
10:16–17).

That which was from the beginning, which we have heard,
which we have seen with our
eyes, which we have looked
upon, and our hands have han-
dled, concerning the Word of life
. . . that which we have seen and
heard we declare to you, that you
also may have fellowship with
us; and truly our fellowship is

with the Father and with His
Son Jesus Christ (1 John 1:1, 3).

_____

_____

Our ministry—the ongoing expression of Christ's life in the world—is so important to God the Father that He sent the Holy Spirit upon Jesus' request to fill us and to enable us to minister. We minister according to the degree that we allow the Holy Spirit to work in us and through us. Our ministry is the ministry of the Holy Spirit. We speak the words, but they are His words. We do the deeds and take the actions and make the decisions, but they are His works that He commands us to do. We are the flesh and bones, the personality and talents. He is the motivation and the life.

Think for a moment about a doctor who ministers to a patient. She does her part. She prescribes the best treatment and medicine she knows. She performs surgery if that is required. Or she sets broken bones or stitches wounds. But only God can heal a sick or injured body. Only God can cause life to overtake disease and death and cause a sick person to become whole again.

The same goes for our work in ministering to others. We do all that we know to do under the direction of the Holy Spirit. But the results of that ministry are His results and His alone. He causes ministry to take root and become a living testimony in our lives.

- *Have you ever had an experience in which you tried to minister to another person solely in your strength and ability? What was the result? How did you feel as you made that effort?*

- *Have you ever had an experience in which you knew you were ministering to another person in the power and strength of the Holy Spirit? What was the result? How did you feel as you engaged in that ministry activity?*

The Giver of Gifts

The Holy Spirit is a giver of many gifts to help us in our ministry. Another way to think of gifts is as enablements or capacities. We can also think of them as helps. The Holy Spirit is described by Jesus as our Helper. He gives us what we need in the form of spiritual gifts to help us accomplish what He asks us to do.

Spiritual gifts are different from our natural gifts and talents—the abilities with which we were born. Natural abilities and talents, along with personality, are gifts of God, but these gifts are given to us in our humanity. They are not divine or spiritual gifts, and they never become spiritual gifts. We err if we believe that our natural gifts automatically become spiritual gifts when we accept Christ Jesus. They do not. Our natural gifts remain after we accept Christ, and they are enhanced or blessed in wonderful ways because of our relationship with Christ Jesus, but they remain as natural, human gifts.

We need to explore, know, develop, and perfect our natural gifts. God has given them to us to use for His kingdom. We should never downplay our abilities; rather, we should develop them to their full potential.

The Holy Spirit adds His unique, divine gifts to our natural talents and abilities. When we combine what He gives us with what has already been given to us, and we seek to use both our natural gifts and the gifts of the Holy Spirit for the Lord's purposes, we truly are serving God with the whole heart, mind, and soul, and we will be the most effective we can be in our contributions to God's kingdom.

- *Have you identified your natural talents and abilities given to you by God?*

———————————————————————————

———————————————————————————

- *In what ways is the Lord challenging you today to use or develop your natural gifts?*

———————————————————————————

———————————————————————————

Gift or Gifts?

The Holy Spirit Himself is the gift of the Father to everyone who believes in Jesus Christ. Paul said to the Corinthians that other believers within the church longed to be with them "because of the exceeding grace of God in you. Thanks be to God for His indescribable gift!" (2 Cor. 9:14–15). That gift is the Holy Spirit, the evidence of God's grace in them.

We receive the Holy Spirit as the supreme Gift, and then He imparts to us of His ability as He wills. We do not receive spiritual gifts apart from the Gift Giver, the Holy Spirit.

The gift of the Spirit is the Holy Spirit Himself. The gifts of the Spirit are the helps, capacities, endowments, enablements that He bestows on us so we might accomplish His purposes.

All of the gifts are resident in and the property of the Holy Spirit. We don't own them. We don't create or manufacture them. We don't grow or produce them. They are His gifts to give.

Types of Spiritual Gifts Given to Believers

These spiritual gifts are given to people who follow Christ Jesus. Just as the Holy Spirit does not indwell those who are nonbelievers, so the gifts of the Holy Spirit are not given to those who have not confessed their sins—accepting what Jesus did on the cross as the substitutionary, sacrificial, all-sufficient atonement for their sins—and received God's forgiveness.

Three classifications of gifts are made to the believers in the New Testament: (1) motivational gifts, (2) gifts given to the church as a whole, and (3) gifts given for specific situations and circumstances. The Holy Spirit gives these gifts to us at His discretion, but He does give gifts to every believer

The Motivational Gifts of the Spirit

The motivational gifts of the Spirit are identified in Romans 12:4–8·

> For as we have many members in one body, but all the members do not have the same function, so we, being many,

are one body in Christ, and individually members of one another. Having then gifts differing according to the grace that is given to us, let us use them: if prophecy, let us prophesy in proportion to our faith; or ministry, let us use it in our ministering; he who teaches, in teaching; he who exhorts, in exhortation; he who gives, with liberality; he who leads, with diligence; he who shows mercy, with cheerfulness.

Every believer has one of the seven motivational gifts described by Paul. I've listed them with some of the meanings or interpretations of these gifts as they appear in other translations of the Bible:

1. *Prophecy*—forthtelling or the speaking out of the truth of God
2. *Ministry*—serving in practical ways (including hospitality, helping, assisting)
3. *Teaching*—explaining the Word of God so that others can understand it and apply it to their lives
4. *Exhortation*—speaking to others in a way that encourages them to follow Christ closely and without hesitation
5. *Giving*—contributing to meet the needs of others
6. *Leadership*—having the ability to administer, govern, and/or rule
7. *Mercy*—giving aid to sick and needy persons (including those who have no merit)

Paul also describes the ways in which we are to use the gifts: prophecy—with faith; ministry and teaching and exhortation—with grace; giving—with generosity; leading—with diligence; and mercy—with cheerfulness.

How do you know which of these gifts you have? Examine your life. When a need is presented or a challenge appears before you in the Lord—a problem arises that you know has a spiritual root or dimension—what is your first response? Do you immediately want to speak the truth? Do you start to serve those who are seeking to provide help, to give, or to organize others? Do you jump in and act with mercy for people who are in need or hurting? Do you respond with words of encouragement that others stay close to the Lord and obey Him explicitly?

- *Have you identified your motivational gift? What is it? How do you feel about having this gift?*

_____

_____

- *In what ways is the Lord challenging you today?*

_____

_____

Gifts Given to the Church

In addition to the endowments that the Holy Spirit gives to individual believers, the Holy Spirit gives gifts to the church as a whole. These gifts are actually people:

> He Himself gave some to be apostles, some prophets, some evangelists, and some pastors and teachers, for the equipping of the saints for the work of ministry, for the edifying of the body of Christ, till we all come to the unity of the faith and of the knowledge of the Son of God, to a perfect man, to the measure of the stature of the fullness of Christ; that we should no longer be children, tossed to and fro and carried about with every wind of doctrine, by the trickery of men, in the cunning craftiness of deceitful plotting, but, speaking the truth in love, may grow up in all things into Him who is the head—Christ (Eph. 4:11–15).

The gifts are given to some in the church. They are the ones called to be

- *apostles*—those who are trailblazers, leaders of new ministry outreaches.
- *prophets*—those who tell the truth of God, including

the ultimate consequences of following or failing to follow God's will.

- *evangelists*—those who proclaim the gospel of Jesus Christ and inspire others to believe in Him.
- *pastors and teachers*—those who nurture, prepare, and teach the believers, equipping them for service to others.

Not every person is called to one of these roles within the church, but in many ways, ministries within a church tend to cluster around these areas of leadership. For example, you may not be called to be a pastor/teacher to a congregation of people, but you may be called by God to serve as a Sunday school teacher. You are operating in the area of ministry as a teacher to the body of Christ, under the leadership of one who is gifted to lead in that area. Or you may serve on an evangelism team. You are serving in the area of evangelism, under the leadership of one who has been gifted to lead in that area.

You will find great fulfillment in serving within the area of ministry to which the Lord calls you. You will find frustration, disappointment, and dissatisfaction in your attempts to serve within an area of ministry to which you are not called to serve by the Holy Spirit.

- *In which area of ministry do you find the Lord leading you to participate with the greatest regularity?*

  _____

  _____

- *How do you feel when you serve in that capacity? How do you feel when you attempt to serve in other areas?*

  _____

  _____

Gifts Unique to Specific Circumstances or Times

The New Testament provides a third set of gifts given to believers by the Holy Spirit. This set of gifts is unique to particular situations and times. In fact, Paul provided this list because he desired to see order restored to the conducting of services in the church at Corinth:

> Now concerning spiritual gifts, brethren, I do not want you to be ignorant. . . . There are diversities of gifts, but the same Spirit. There are differences of ministries, but the same Lord. And there are diversities of activities, but it is the same God who works all in all. But the manifestation of the Spirit is given to each one for the profit of all: for to one is given the word of wisdom through the Spirit, to another the word of knowledge through the same Spirit, to another faith by the same Spirit, to another gifts of healings by the same Spirit, to another the working of miracles, to another prophecy, to another discerning of spirits, to another different kinds of tongues, to another the interpretation of tongues. But one and the same Spirit works all these things, distributing to each one individually as He wills. For as the body is one and has many members, but all the members of that one body, being many, are one body, so also is Christ. For by one Spirit we were all baptized into one body—whether Jews or Greeks, whether slaves or free—and have all been made to drink into one Spirit (1 Cor. 12:1, 4–13).

Paul's primary concern was not with the listing of gifts, but with the point that there is only one Holy Spirit. The Corinthians had been idol worshipers. As pagan Greeks prior to their conversion to Christ Jesus, they had a different god for each activity, enterprise, and object. Athens, for example, was filled with thousands of idols, each with a specific identity and purpose. Some idol gods were more valued than others. Paul wanted the Corinthians to make certain they understood that there is only one Holy Spirit— He manifests Himself in different ways through different individuals as He wills.

The gifts that Paul cited are specific to particular times and events. As the church would gather, different gifts might be manifested depending on the needs of the people and the problems in the church at that time. Paul wanted them to understand that all of the gifts come from the same Holy Spirit, with no one gift having a claim on being the definitive manifestation of the Spirit's presence in their midst.

These gifts are bestowed on the believers so that one person may be given one gift and another person another gift. All of the gifts are possible, but none of them are assured in any one setting or group of people. In like manner, no one person has his or her identity associated with a particular gift. In other words, one person is not expected to be the prophet at all meetings, and another person the one who gives a word of wisdom. The Holy Spirit speaks and works through this one, and that one, and another one at His direction and for His purposes.

The conclusion we must draw, therefore, is that a believer may experience one or more of these gifts operating in and through him during his lifetime, but not necessarily with any predictability or regularity. Why? Because the Holy Spirit orchestrates His particular set of gifts to be in operation in each group of people depending on the needs in the group.

The Corinthians apparently had a fondness and desire for the more dramatic gifts, such as healing, tongues, working of miracles. Paul admonished them in 1 Corinthians 13 that love is far more important than spiritual gifts, and then in 1 Corinthians 14, he admonished them to desire prophecy as the foremost gift to seek, so they might speak the truth of God with clarity to nonbelievers and believers alike.

Consider also the words of Paul below. What light do they shed on his statement to the Corinthians that the "one and the same Spirit works all these things, distributing to each one individually as He wills" (v. 11)?

What the Word Says	What the Word Says to Me
You know that you were Gentiles, carried away to these dumb idols, however you were led.	_____ _____ _____

Therefore I make known to you
that no one speaking by the
Spirit of God calls Jesus ac-
cursed, and no one can say that
Jesus is Lord except by the Holy
Spirit (1 Cor. 12:2–3).

Are all apostles? Are all prophets? Are all teachers? Are all
workers of miracles? Do all have
gifts of healing? Do all speak
with tongues? Do all interpret?
But earnestly desire the best gifts
(1 Cor. 12:29–31).

Though I speak with the tongues
of men and of angels, but have
not love, I have become sounding
brass or a clanging cymbal. And
though I have the gift of prophecy, and understand all mysteries
and all knowledge, and though I
have all faith, so that I could remove mountains, but have not
love, I am nothing. And though I
bestow all my goods to feed the
poor, and though I give my body
to be burned, but have not love,
it profits me nothing (1 Cor.
13:1–3).

A Unique Blend

How do all of these gifts fit together for the individual believer?
First, you must discern your motivational gift and operate in it.
Then, you must follow the leading of the Holy Spirit as He calls

you to a particular area of ministry within the church. As you use your motivational gift in ministry within the church, you must continually make yourself available to the Spirit to manifest Himself in you and through you with one or more of the spiritual gifts in 1 Corinthians 12.

God knows who you are. He knows who He created you to be and which natural gifts, talents, abilities, and personality traits He put into your life. He knows which motivational gift is best suited to you.

God knows how to place us within a body of people to accomplish His ministry. He will open doors of opportunity for you to minister in a way that is suited to your natural gifts and your motivational gift.

Finally, God knows His master plan for this world and what is needed to fulfill it at any second in history. He knows the people He needs in which areas of ministry at which times and places, and for which purposes. Therefore, He knows which specific spiritual gift is necessary at any given time for the accomplishing of His purposes.

The Holy Spirit is the giver of these gifts, and they are always given at His discretion and for His purposes. Be open to how and when the Holy Spirit chooses to use you.

- *What new insights do you have about the Holy Spirit's bestowal of spiritual gifts?*

  _____

  _____

- *In what ways is the Lord challenging you today?*

  _____

  _____

LESSON 9

RELYING ON THE HOLY SPIRIT TO MAKE OUR MINISTRIES EFFECTIVE

In the last lesson, we discussed the unique blend of spiritual gifts that the Holy Spirit bestows on various believers in Christ Jesus. In this lesson we are going to focus on the reasons that the Holy Spirit gives us these gifts.

There are four main reasons for the bestowal of spiritual gifts in our lives:

1. They are for the common good of all believers.
2. They equip us for further ministry.
3. They are for our encouragement.
4. They are for our edification.

Ultimately, all of the gifts are intended to be manifested so that Jesus Christ is lifted up and God the Father is glorified. Anytime the spiritual gifts call attention to us, the ones who are manifesting these gifts, we are in error. All spiritual gifts belong to God and come from Him, and all praise for the results or benefits of these gifts should be directed to God.

Furthermore, we are to hold these gifts and to use them as good stewards of God's grace. We are to recognize at all times that we didn't create these gifts or authorize their use, and therefore, we have no right to lay claim to them. We are to use them wisely for the purpose that their true owner, the Holy Spirit, intended. The servant may use the master's utensils, china, and silverware to prepare and serve a magnificent meal for the benefit of the master's guests, but the servant does not own the utensils, china, and silverware. In like manner, we employ the gifts of the Spirit for the benefit of others.

This does not mean that we are to take the bestowal of spiritual gifts lightly. We are to cherish them, hold them in high regard, and manifest them in our lives with boldness, confidence, and dignity. Peter wrote,

> As each one has received a gift, minister it to one another, as good stewards of the manifold grace of God. If anyone speaks, let him speak as the oracles of God. If anyone ministers, let him do it as with the ability which God supplies, that in all things God may be glorified through Jesus Christ, to whom belong the glory and the dominion forever and ever (1 Peter 4:10–11).

The gifts that we receive from the Holy Spirit are for us to use, manifest, or employ for the benefit of others. Freely we have received of the Spirit, and freely we give. (See Matt. 10:8.) What we receive from God we are expected to share with others for their benefit more than for our benefit. We, in turn, receive from others the benefit from the gifts that the Holy Spirit gives to them. In this way, we are formed into a body of believers and are built up as a community of faith.

For the Common Good

The gifts are intended to be used "for the profit of all" (1 Cor. 12:7). When one hurts in the body of Christ, all are hurt. When one is blessed, all are blessed. The gifts are intended to bring healing, wholeness, and benefit to a body of believers.

The motivational gift you receive from the Holy Spirit is given *to* you, but it is *for* others. (See Rom. 12:4–7—prophecy, ministry, teaching, exhortation, giving, leadership, mercy.) If you are given a role in the church, your ministry gift is for service to others. (See Eph. 4:11—apostle, prophet, evangelist, pastor, teacher.) If you are given a spiritual gift, you are to manifest it and help others. (See 1 Cor. 12:7–10—word of wisdom, word of knowledge, faith, healings, miracles, prophecy, discerning of spirits, tongues, interpretation of tongues.)

Always ask yourself, How can I use this gift for the common good?

- *What new insights do you have about the purpose of the Holy Spirit's gifts in enabling you for effective ministry?*

  _____

  _____

- *In what ways is the Lord challenging you today?*

  _____

  _____

For Equipping the Saints

Recall that Ephesians 4:11–12 tells us that the gifts to the church—the placing of apostles, prophets, evangelists, pastors, and teachers within the church—are for this purpose: "equipping of the saints for the work of ministry." The purpose of a good sermon is to inspire the congregation to be obedient and faithful in their walk with the Lord. The purpose of a good Bible lesson is to help people grow in faith and in their understanding about how to apply the Bible to their lives.

Paul also wrote to the Ephesians, "We are His workmanship, created in Christ Jesus for good works, which God prepared beforehand that we should walk in them" (Eph. 2:10). You are God's masterpiece. He has saved you, gifted you with natural abilities and talents, preserved and protected and provided for you, and now, through the Holy Spirit, He has given you spiritual gifts. At the same time, He has prepared a place for you to use the gifts. Even as the Lord was preparing you to serve in His church, He was preparing others to be in position to receive what you have to give to them. He has paved the way for your ministry to be effective. In other words, others need what the Holy Spirit prompts you to prepare and give to them. You, in turn, need what others have been prompted by the Holy Spirit to give to you.

When we truly begin to see that every person who crosses our path has been allowed to cross our path by the Holy Spirit, for a purpose that has benefit to us—a benefit that may be of learning, growing, cleansing, healing—what a marvelous adventure we experience in daily living! Furthermore, if a believer crosses our path, that believer has been put there by the Holy Spirit for the express purpose of equipping us in some way for the work of ministry. There is something we are to learn or acquire from every conversation, every encounter, with another saint of God.

- *How does this make you feel as a believer in Christ Jesus? Can you recall an experience when the Lord put someone in your path to equip you in some way for a more effective ministry?*

_____

_____

- *In what ways is the Lord challenging you today?*

_____

_____

For Encouragement of the Believers

We need encouragement in our lives on a daily basis. We need someone to build us up and help us see our value and worth before the Lord. The devil and the world's systems grind us down and wear us out. We need others in the body of Christ to remind us that we are God's unique and irreplaceable creations, called to unique and irreplaceable places of ministry. We need to be reminded of God's love for us and of our importance to the church.

Paul addressed this need for encouragement in his letter to the Corinthians:

> If the foot should say, "Because I am not a hand, I am not of the body," is it therefore not of the body? And if the ear should say, "Because I am not an eye, I am not of the body," is it therefore not of the body? If the whole body were an eye, where would be the hearing? If the whole were hearing, where would be the smelling? But now God has set the members, each one of them, in the body just as He pleased. And if they were all one member, where would the body be? But now indeed there are many members, yet one body. And the eye cannot say to the hand, "I have no need of you"; nor again the head to the feet, "I have no need of you." No, much rather, those members of the body which seem to be weaker are necessary. And those members of the body which we think to be less honorable, on these we bestow greater honor; and our unpresentable parts have greater modesty, but our presentable parts have no need. But God composed the body, having given greater honor to that part which lacks it, that there should be no schism in the body, but that the members should have the same care for one another. And if one member suffers, all the members suffer with it; or if one member is honored, all the members rejoice with it (1 Cor. 12:15–26).

As the gifts of the Spirit are shared among believers, under the direction and orchestration of the Spirit, we can't help having an awareness that God counts each of us as highly valuable in His church. No matter what our social status, profession, or lot in life may be, we can be used by the Holy Spirit in valuable roles of ministry.

You may say, "I don't see how God can use me. I'm totally inadequate." Or you may say, "I can't be used by God. I'll fail."

That's not what God says. He says, "Let me use you. I'll use whatever you do and I'll be in whatever you do, and that means it will be a blessing to someone. I never fail, and since I'm in whatever good you do for My body, whatever you do won't fail."

Your spiritual gifts should always bring encouragement to others. Even if you have a motivational gift of exhortation, the ultimate purpose of exhortation is to say to another person, "You *can* follow Christ. You can walk in obedience and righteousness before Him." If you operate in the gift of evangelism, exercise your gift in such a way that people hear the good news that Jesus came to save them from their sins, not that a hell is waiting to swallow them up. If you give a word of wisdom to another person, that word of wisdom is to give her direction that points her toward God and toward His answers in her life. Such a word will automatically point them away from danger and sin, but it should do so as an encouraging word to receive God's best in her life.

- *What new insights do you have into the nature of God's gifts and how they relate to our ministries?*

  _____

  _____

- *In what ways is the Lord challenging you in your exercise of spiritual gifts?*

  _____

  _____

For Edification

Spiritual gifts are to be exercised or manifested for the edification of the church. *Edification* means the "building up" or the "strengthening" of the church. Paul wrote, "Since you are zealous for spiritual gifts, let it be for the edification of the church that you seek to excel" (1 Cor. 14:12).

All things are to be done so that the church body as a whole might be perfected—so that sin might be cleansed from the midst of a group of believers, so that healing and wholeness might occur individually and collectively, so that conflicts might be resolved and relationships reconciled, so that losses might be restored and excesses trimmed away.

In writing about the gifts to the church, Paul gave an outline of what edification produces. (See Eph. 4:13–15.) A thoroughly edified group of believers would have this profile:

- Unity of the faith and of the knowledge of the Son of God
- Manifesting the fullness of Christ
- No longer tossed to and fro by the wind of every doctrine that comes to town
- No longer deceived by the trickery of men
- No longer engaged in deceitful plotting or cunning craftiness
- Speaking the truth in love

Paul concluded that the end result of edification is a "whole body"—one that is "joined and knit together by what every joint supplies, according to the effective working by which every part does its share" (Eph. 4:16). As with the manifestation of spiritual gifts, this process is to be marked by love (v. 16).

As you think back over your motivational gifts and your role of ministry within the church, ask yourself, Am I manifesting the gifts of the Spirit in such a way that the entire body of Christ is built up? Are my gifts contributing toward our perfection as a group of believers in Christ Jesus?

- *Recall an experience that left you feeling edified. How does it feel to be edified? What was the lasting effect in your life?*

_____

_____

- *In what ways is the Lord challenging you today in your exercise of the Holy Spirit's gifts?*

_____

_____

Lasting Benefits

When the gifts of the Holy Spirit are manifested in ministry that is for the common good, that equips the saints for further ministry, that is marked by encouragement, and that results in edification, they bless now, and they bless forever.

Paul declared to the Corinthians, "We are God's fellow workers; you are God's field, you are God's building." He followed that statement with these sobering words:

> According to the grace of God which was given to me, as a wise master builder I have laid the foundation, and another builds on it. But let each one take heed how he builds on it. For no other foundation can anyone lay than that which is laid, which is Jesus Christ. Now if anyone builds on this foundation with gold, silver, precious stones, wood, hay, straw, each one's work will become clear; for the Day will declare it, because it will be revealed by fire; and the fire will test each one's work, of what sort it is. If anyone's work which he has built on it endures, he will receive a reward. If anyone's work is burned, he will suffer loss; but he himself will be saved, yet so as through fire (1 Cor. 3:9–15).

Your use of the Holy Spirit's gifts in ministry is not just for the here and now. They should have an eternal ring to them, and they will if they truly are gifts from the Holy Spirit. When you invite the Holy Spirit to be the director of your ministry efforts, when you invite the Holy Spirit to work through you to bless others, He will do so. He is eternal. And whatever He does in and through you will have an eternal quality to it.

If you truly desire to minister in effective ways, you must desire for your ministry to last for all eternity. That can happen only as you allow the Holy Spirit to help you in any act of ministry you undertake. It can happen only as you regard each spiritual gift as coming from Him and being used for the perfecting of His body.

- *What new insights do you have into the nature of the Holy Spirit, the purpose of His gifts in our lives, and how to use your spiritual gifts in ministry?*

- *In what specific ways do you feel the Lord challenging you today?*

LESSON 10

RELYING ON THE HOLY SPIRIT FOR DAILY GUIDANCE

To whom do you turn for daily guidance in how to live your life, what to do, where to go, whom to see, how to make decisions and choices? The Scriptures tell us that the only Guide worth having in our lives is the Holy Spirit. He is the only One who knows our past completely from the moment we were conceived to this present day, knows our future completely, from this day extending into eternity, and knows God's plan and purpose for us today and each day of our lives.

When we turn to people for advice, we must be aware that in many cases, they will tell us only what they think we want to hear. They likely desire to make us feel good so we will like them more, which in turn makes them feel good. If you seek advice from another person, get advice that is honest, true to God's Word, and without ulterior motive.

Even as you receive advice from others, you must check it against the Holy Spirit's witness in your spirit and against the Bible to verify that the advice you have heard is the right advice for you in your given circumstance.

Only the Holy Spirit knows what is fully good and right for you on a daily basis. Any other opinion can be only a part of the full truth, which is known by the Holy Spirit.

In John 14—16, Jesus refers to the Holy Spirit repeatedly as the Spirit of truth. Note in the verses below what He says about the Holy Spirit's manifestation of truth in your life.

What the Word Says	What the Word Says to Me
The Spirit of truth . . . dwells with you and will be in you. I will not leave you orphans; I will come to you (John 14:17).	_____ _____ _____ _____
The Spirit of truth who proceeds from the Father, He will testify of Me (John 15:26).	_____ _____ _____
He will guide you into all truth; for He will not speak on His own authority, but whatever He hears He will speak; and He will tell you things to come (John 16:13).	_____ _____ _____ _____ _____
He will glorify Me, for He will take of what is Mine and declare it to you (John 16:14).	_____ _____ _____

The Spirit of truth is like an inner compass in our lives—always pointing us toward what Jesus would be, say, or do in any given moment or circumstance.

God Has Always Sought to Guide His People

Daily guidance is not something that was initiated by Jesus in His sending the Holy Spirit to us. Guidance has been God's desire for His people throughout the ages. Numerous verses in the Old

Testament point toward God's guidance of His people. Certainly, He provided daily guidance for His people as they left Egypt and crossed the wilderness to the land God had promised to them. His guidance then was manifested as a pillar of cloud by day and a pillar of fire by night. (Recall that the symbol of fire is usually associated with the Holy Spirit.)

As you read the verses below, consider how the Lord is seeking to guide you as His child today.

What the Word Says	What the Word Says to Me
The LORD is my shepherd; I shall not want. He makes me to lie down in green pastures; He leads me beside the still waters (Ps. 23:1–2).	
Trust in the LORD with all your heart, And lean not on your own understanding; In all your ways acknowledge Him, And He shall direct your paths (Prov. 3:5–6).	
Your ears shall hear a word behind you, saying, "This is the way, walk in it," Whenever you turn to the right hand Or whenever you turn to the left (Isa. 30:21).	

God desires to make His will known to you. He wants you to

know what to do and when to do it. Trust the Holy Spirit to be your daily Guide.

Throughout the Gospels, we have a strong sense that Jesus was guided on a daily basis by the Holy Spirit. After the Holy Spirit was poured out on the disciples of Jesus, they, too, were led in profound ways by the Holy Spirit. The verses below are just a few examples of how the Holy Spirit dealt with His people in ways that provided very personal and specific guidance. What He did for them then, He desires to do for you now.

What the Word Says	What the Word Says to Me
Then the Spirit told me to go with them, doubting nothing (Acts 11:12).	_____ _____ _____
As they ministered to the Lord and fasted, the Holy Spirit said, "Now separate to Me Barnabas and Saul for the work to which I have called them" (Acts 13:2).	_____ _____ _____ _____ _____
Now when they had gone through Phrygia and the region of Galatia, they were forbidden by the Holy Spirit to preach the word in Asia (Acts 16:6).	_____ _____ _____ _____ _____

The leaders of the early church relied on the Holy Spirit to give them this kind of specific, personal guidance, and we are wise to do likewise.

Both Romans 8:14 and Galatians 5:18 refer to our being "led by the Spirit." This is considered to be the norm of the Christian life.

What Are the Results of His Guidance?

The Scriptures describe at least three wonderful results of the Holy Spirit's guidance in our lives.

1. He will convict of sin, of righteousness, and of judgment (John 16:8). The Holy Spirit gives us a very clear understanding of what is wrong, what is right, and how to tell wrong from right. He reveals the truth of any situation to us to keep us from stumbling or from entering into error. He truly "delivers us from evil" in this way. (See Matt. 6:13.)

2. He will help us "walk circumspectly, not as fools but as wise, redeeming the time, because the days are evil" (Eph. 5:15–16). He will lead us to right choices, right relationships, and right priorities so we might enjoy the maximum fulfillment we can experience in our lives. He will help us make the most of our time each day.

3. He searches our hearts (Rom. 8:27). He reveals to us our deepest motives and desires.

In so doing, the Holy Spirit shows us who we really are and how we can become more like Jesus. He gives us guidance to help us make the choices that will help us mature in the Lord and become more like Jesus day by day.

- *Can you recall an experience in which you received the personal, specific guidance of the Holy Spirit? What was the result? How did it feel to receive the guidance of the Holy Spirit?*

  _____

  _____

- *In what ways is the Holy Spirit challenging you today?*

  _____

  _____

Conditions for the Spirit's Guidance

You may ask, "Are there any conditions placed upon the guidance of the Holy Spirit in our lives?"

Yes.

First, we must believe in Jesus. We must accept Him as our personal Savior, confess our sins, and receive God's forgiveness. The Holy Spirit does not give daily guidance to nonbelievers. The only direction that the Holy Spirit gives to nonbelievers is the conviction that they need to accept Christ Jesus.

Second, we must stay yielded to the Spirit. We must say yes to the Spirit when He prompts us to take a certain action or say a certain word. We must give mental assent to the Spirit's direction, and we must actually obey His prompting and follow through in doing or saying what He has called us to do or say.

How can you know if you are yielded to the Holy Spirit? You are yielded to Him when you can say to Him, "Here is what I desire. But if Your answer is no to this, it's all right. I'll do what You say."

Third, we must believe for His guidance. We must expect the Holy Spirit to speak in the inner person and direct us toward good and away from evil. We must be intentional and focused in this. We are much more likely to hear what the Holy Spirit has to say to us if we are actively listening for Him to speak. We are much more likely to see the Holy Spirit's direction if we are looking for His signs. Hebrews 11:6 tells us that God is a "rewarder of those who diligently seek Him." We are to be diligent in seeking His guidance, asking for it, watching for it, anticipating it, and receiving it.

Fourth, we are to wait upon the Lord until we receive His guidance. Psalm 27:14 tells us,

> *Wait on the LORD;*
> *Be of good courage,*
> *And He shall strengthen your heart;*
> *Wait, I say, on the LORD!*

Until the Lord tells you what role you are to play, don't act. If you don't know what to say, stay and pray. If you don't know where to turn, don't get up from your knees.

Don't become impatient in your desire to hear from the Lord or to receive His guidance. Wait. Listen. His guidance will come.

- *In what ways is the Lord challenging you today?*

_____

_____

How Guidance Is Imparted to Us

The Holy Spirit imparts His truth to us—His daily guidance to us—primarily in these ways:

He speaks to us through the words of the Bible. The Spirit will never lead you to do anything that is contrary to God's Word. If you believe you have heard the Lord speak in your heart, go to the Word of God to confirm that message. Very often as we are reading God's Word, He speaks in our hearts, "Do this. This is for you. That's My desire for you." He quickens certain passages or verses to us.

Now we can always find a phrase or verse in the Bible to back up what we desire to do in our human nature. I am not at all suggesting that you go to the Bible to "get a verse" as justification for the decision you've already chosen to make. That's not being led by the Spirit.

Rather, I'm recommending that you read your Bible daily with this prayer on your lips: "Holy Spirit, speak to me through the Word. Just as You inspired men of old to write these words, inspire me to apply these words to my life."

He gives us the principles of the Word of God to guide us in making decisions. In many cases, there isn't a specific story or passage of Scripture that seems to speak directly to our situation. But the principles of God's Word are true and eternal. They can be applied to give us guidance in making choices and decisions. Consider the verses below as they apply to decision making.

What the Word Says	What the Word Says to Me
Whatever you do, do all to the glory of God (1 Cor. 10:31).	_____ _____
Giving thanks always for all things to God the Father in the name of our Lord Jesus Christ (Eph. 5:20).	_____ _____ _____ _____

Whatever you do in word or
deed, do all in the name of the
Lord Jesus (Col. 3:17).

_____
_____
_____

In everything by prayer and supplication, with thanksgiving, let
your requests be made known to
God; and the peace of God,
which surpasses all understanding, will guard your hearts
and minds through Christ Jesus
(Phil. 4:6–7).

_____
_____
_____
_____
_____
_____
_____

If you can answer yes to these questions about a decision or choice you are about to make, you are making your decision within the principles of God's Word: Will God be glorified in this? Can I give thanks to God for this? Can I do this in the name of Jesus, fully expecting His blessing, His provision, and His stamp of approval? When I pray about this, do I feel God's peace in my heart?

He speaks to us through circumstances. As we wait upon the Lord and trust Him for guidance, the Spirit very often opens certain doors in our lives and closes other doors: "All things work together for good to those who love God, to those who are the called according to His purpose" (Rom. 8:28). We must believe for this verse to be true in our lives and be willing to watch and see how the Lord moves in the lives of others and how He brings resolution to situations that have seemed impossible to resolve.

He speaks to us in the stillness of our hearts with a word of conviction or assurance. When the Holy Spirit is directing us away from something harmful to us, we very often have a heaviness or a feeling of trouble, foreboding, or uneasiness in our spirits. When the Holy Spirit is directing us toward things that are helpful to us, we tend to feel a deep inner peace, an eagerness to see what God will do, and a feeling of joy.

A Complete Guidance

The Holy Spirit often works predominantly through one of these methods to give us guidance, but His complete guidance is usually confirmed as He uses *all* of these methods to speak His truth to us. We read something in the Word that speaks to us. We are reminded of general principles in God's Word, and we begin to see how they apply to our situation—perhaps through the message of a song or a sermon, the words of a friend, or a sudden recollection of passages we have read in God's Word previously. We see circumstances beginning to change around us. We feel the presence of the Spirit in our lives convicting us to turn from evil or His assurance that we can embrace fully something that will be for our good.

The Holy Spirit does not desire that God's will for our lives be a mystery to us. He has come to reveal the truth to us. He has come in His all-knowing ability to impart to us what we need to know in order to live obedient and faithful lives. Trust Him to guide you, now and always!

- *Recall an experience in which you have received the guidance of the Holy Spirit. How did He speak to you? How did He confirm His direction in your life?*

  _____

  _____

- *How does it feel to be guided by the Holy Spirit?*

  _____

  _____

- *What new insights do you have into the way the Holy Spirit guides us?*

  _____

  _____

- *In what ways is the Lord challenging you today?*

  _____

  _____

MY FINAL WORD TO YOU

*T*he *Spirit-filled life.* I opened this Bible study with those words, and I want to close with them. But let me add the word *wonderful* to this phrase: *the wonderful Spirit-filled life.*

The life that the Holy Spirit desires to impart to you—and to live within you and through you—can be described only as wonderful. Wonderful in the many benefits we experience personally. Wonderful in the many blessings that come to others around us. Wonderful in the sense that we are made more keenly aware of the glory and majesty of God the Father and Jesus Christ, His Son.

The Spirit-filled life should be marked by awe that we should be so privileged as to be indwelled by the Holy Spirit of almighty God, who desires to use us in accomplishing His purposes on this earth and who desires to live with us forever in eternity.

The extent to which you live a Spirit-led life is up to you. Choose today to rely on the Holy Spirit for every aspect of your life, in every decision or choice you make, during every hour of every day. Trust Him to work in you and through you. Trust Him to mold you and make you into the image of Christ Jesus. Trust Him to bless you as you have never been blessed before.

As you ask Him to do His work in and through your life, you will receive His help and guidance. And in the process, you will manifest His character.

ABOUT THE AUTHOR

Charles Stanley is pastor of the 13,000-member First Baptist Church in Atlanta, Georgia. He is the speaker on the internationally popular radio and television program *In Touch*.

Twice elected president of the Southern Baptist Convention, Stanley received his bachelor of arts degree from the University of Richmond, his bachelor of divinity degree from Southwestern Theological Seminary, and his master's and doctor's degrees from Luther Rice Seminary.

Dr. Stanley is the author of many books, including *The Glorious Journey, The Source of My Strength, The Wonderful Spirit-Filled Life, The Gift of Forgiveness, How to Listen to God, Winning the War Within,* and *How to Handle Adversity.*

Books by Charles Stanley
from Thomas Nelson Publishers

Eternal Security

Dr. Stanley offers the powerful, reassuring message that believers can be certain of eternal salvation and know peace and intimacy with Christ as a result.

The Gift of Forgiveness

Dr. Stanley shows readers how to give and receive forgiveness and experience the healing and freedom forgiveness brings.

The Glorious Journey

Dr. Stanley provides crucial answers to contemporary questions and concerns along with a thoroughly biblical understanding of the foundational issues of the faith.

How to Handle Adversity

Reassuring, Bible-based advice on how to understand and handle adversity in ways that glorify God and demonstrate His faithfulness.

How to Keep Your Kids on Your Team

Brimming with wisdom and practical advice, this book is a must for all Christian parents who want to ensure that their children grow to be loving and loyal.

How to Listen to God

Dr. Stanley's most popular book provides direction for Christians who are struggling to hear God's voice and to understand His will for their lives.

The In Touch Study Series
A unique series of study guides that invites readers to study the Scriptures in light of their past experience, current emotional response, possible future application, and Spirit-prompted conviction.

Listening to God
Experience a deeper relationship with God by learning to hear His voice.

Advancing Through Adversity
Learn to grow through difficult times and rediscover God's faithfulness.

Experiencing Forgiveness
Enjoy the peace that comes from giving and receiving it.

Relying on the Holy Spirit
Experience the joy-filled walk with God under the anointing of the Holy Spirit.

The Source of My Strength
Sharing his own journey through emotional pain, Dr. Stanley encourages readers to face the hurts of the past and receive God's healing and freedom.

Winning the War Within
A reasoned, scriptural approach to triumphing over temptation and coping with trials and inner struggles.

The Wonderful Spirit-Filled Life
Dr. Stanley gives believers the keys to living an abundant life, deepening their personal relationship with Christ, and applying biblical truths.